Englisch

9./10. Klasse

Astrid Stannat, Martina Mattes

If-Sätze und Futurformen

Mit heraustrennbarem Lösungsteil

Mentor Übungsbuch 856

Mentor Verlag München

Die Autorinnen: Astrid Stannat, Martina Mattes, Gymnasiallehrerinnen und Autorinnen mehrerer didaktischer Werke für Englisch

Redaktion: Ulrike Timmer

Illustrationen: Henning Schöttke, Kiel

In neuer Rechtschreibung

Umwelthinweis: Gedruckt auf chlorfrei gebleichtem Papier

Layout: Peter Glaubitz, auf der Basis des Layouts von Barbara Slowik, München
Umschlag: Iris Steiner, München
Satz: OK Satz GmbH, Unterschleißheim
Druck: Landesverlag Druckservice, Linz

Printed in Austria • ISBN 3-580-63856-4

1. 2. 3. 4. 5. 05 04 03 02 01

Inhaltsverzeichnis

Unser Tipp für alle, die noch mehr wissen wollen:

Mentor Lernhilfen

Die sind Spezialisten im Erklären und machen fit fürs ganze Schuljahr!

Für Englisch in der 9./10. Klasse gibt's die Bände:

The Final Touch 1 (9./10. Klasse)
Indirekte Rede, Gerundium, Infinitiv, Artikel, Adjektiv, Adverb
ISBN 3-580-63550-6

The Final Touch 2 (9./10. Klasse)
Relativsätze, Pluralformen, Hilfsverben, Partizip, Simple Past, Present Perfect, Verlaufsform
ISBN 3-580-63551-4

Vorwort

V

Hallo, liebe Schülerin, lieber Schüler,

du möchtest dein Englisch ein bisschen trainieren, aber möglichst gezielt und mit Erfolg? Dann bist du hier richtig – egal, ob du dich nun generell verbessern oder eines der Themen dieses Buches speziell üben willst.

Und so funktioniert's:

Treffsicher — Dieses Buch ist in **24 kleine Lernportionen** gegliedert.
→ So findest du dich besonders schnell zurecht.

Übersichtlich — Jede Lernportion umfasst genau eine **Doppelseite**.
→ So hast du immer alles auf einen Blick.

Einleuchtend — Jede Doppelseite beginnt mit einer kurzen, klaren **Regel**.
→ So weißt du immer sofort, worauf es ankommt.

Clever — Dann geht's ans **Üben** – ganz locker, Schritt für Schritt.
→ So bereitest du dich optimal vor.

Praktisch — Der **Lösungsteil** zum Heraustrennen passt seitengetreu dazu.
→ So kontrollierst du blitzschnell – ohne Suchen und Blättern.

Am besten gleich loslegen!

Viel Spaß und ganz viel Erfolg
wünscht dir
dein Mentor Verlag

Noch ein Tipp — Du hast noch mehr Nachholbedarf, aber keine Lust auf Nachhilfe? Dann versuch's doch mit den **Mentor Lernhilfen**: Schau mal auf die Seite gegenüber!

A Warming up

1. Die Zeiten: Simple Present, Simple Past, Past Perfect

Die Bildung dieser Zeiten solltest du sicher beherrschen, bevor du dich mit den if-Sätzen beschäftigst:

Simple Present

Positive sentence:	Negative sentence:
→ *I **like** ice-cream.*	→ *I **don't like** spinach.*
→ *John **likes** ice-cream.*	→ *John **doesn't like** spinach.*

Simple Past

Positive sentence:	Negative sentence:
→ *Sarah **washed** her hands.*	→ *She **didn't wash** her hair.*
→ *We **went** by car.*	→ *We **didn't go** by bike.*

Past Perfect

Positive sentence:	Negative sentence:
→ *Tom **had seen** the film before.*	→ *He **hadn't seen** the original version.*
→ *Sally and Ben **had stayed** for three days.*	→ *They **hadn't stayed** till Sunday.*

Übung 1

Kevin is reading the TV guide for the weekend.
Fill in the present tense forms of the verbs and decide whether or not you have to add -s.

Air Force One:
In this thriller Harrison Ford .... (play) the US President who .... (find) himself trapped on board a hijacked plane.

The Full Monty:
This smash hit movie is about a group of unemployed Sheffield steel workers who .... (turn) to stripping to escape the poverty trap.

McLeod's Daughters:
Set in the Australian outback, this drama .... (trace) the fortunes of a daughter who .... (return) to the family farm when her father .... (die).

One Fine Day:
George Clooney and Michelle Pfeiffer .... (star, *dt. die Hauptrolle spielen*) as two single parents who .... (get) through a series of chaotic events.

Übung 2

Samantha found an article about her favourite TV series *Emergency Room.*
Fill in the correct simple past forms of the verbs in brackets.

A million female hearts .... (break) when they .... (come) out last year with the news that Dr Doug Ross (George Clooney) would be quitting County General Hospital at the end of the fifth serial. Clooney .... (decide) to concentrate on his big screen career (*dt. Leinwand-, Kinokarriere*).
When the British actress Alex Kingston was offered a role in *Emergency Room*, she .... (not find) it easy to move to America. While Alex .... (be) unsure, *Emergency Room's* producers .... (not be). "When she .... (walk) in, she .... (show) such intelligence and humour that we .... (not hesitate) one minute."
At first Alex .... (not like) Los Angeles. "But my colleagues really .... (help) me. They are wonderful actors and there's a lot of laughter around the set. They .... (make) me feel at home."

Übung 3

Samantha had written a long list of things she wanted to do at the weekend. Write down what she had already done and what she had not done yet when her friend Sheila phoned her on Sunday.

send an e-mail to Sabine ✓
repair my bike
buy some ice-cream ✓
write an essay for school ✓
learn German words
tidy up my room
make a cake ✓

When Sheila phoned her on Sunday, Samantha had already sent an e-mail to Sabine, her German friend. She hadn't repaired her bike yet.

....

....

....

....

....

....

A 2. Regelmäßige und unregelmäßige Verben

Bei den unregelmäßigen Verben lernst du immer drei Formen, z. B. ***go* – *went* – *gone*.**

Die 1. Form entspricht dem **Infinitive** (Grundform): ***go*** (gehen). Du brauchst sie für bejahte und verneinte Sätze in der Gegenwart. Achtung: In der 3. Person Singular muss ein *-s* angehängt werden: ***I walk – I don't walk; she walks – she doesn't walk***

Die 2. Form entspricht dem **Simple Past** (1. Vergangenheit): ***went*** (ging).
Achtung: Die verneinte Form wird mit *didn't* + Infinitiv gebildet: ***he didn't go***

Die 3. Form enspricht dem **Past Participle** (Partizip Perfekt). Sie wird für die zusammengesetzten Zeiten, wie z. B. das Past Perfect, benötigt: *he had* ***gone*** (er war gegangen)

Bei den regelmäßigen Verben lauten die 2. und die 3. Form gleich:
paint – painted – painted
skip – skipped – skipped
tidy up – tidied up – tidied up

Übung 1

Complete the table with the correct verb forms.

Simple Present	**Simple Past**	**Past Perfect**
he solves	he solved	he had solved
....	we didn't take	....
they think	....	....
....	you emptied	....
....	....	she hadn't given
I don't stop	....	....
....	he helped	....
....	....	she had seen
we move	....	....

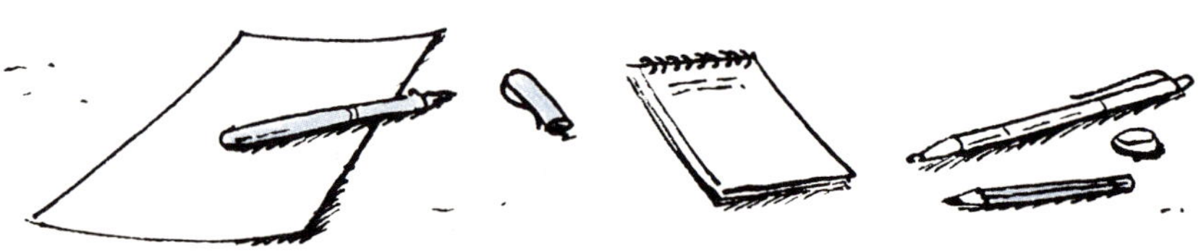

Übung 2 **Last summer Kevin went to Malta with his parents and his sister Fiona.**
Fill in the missing verb forms. Use the tense given in brackets.

After they .... (pick up: *past perfect*) their luggage, a bus .... (take: *simple past*) them to their hotel. They .... (have: *simple past*) rooms with a beautiful view of the sea.

After they .... (spend: *past perfect*) their first day on the beach, they .... (realize: *simple past*) that they all .... (turn: *past perfect*) quite red in the hot summer sun. They .... (not use: *past perfect*) any sunscreen product for their skin – a mistake they .... (not make: *simple past*) again!

Mrs Northam .... (love: *simple present*) going to museums. On Sunday they .... (visit: *simple past*) Malta's capital Valetta. Kevin and Fiona .... (not want: *simple past*) to spend hours at the National Museum with their parents, so they .... (go: *simple past*) to a café instead.

Fiona .... (not like: *simple present*) history at school very much, but she .... (be: *simple past*) very impressed by the prehistoric temples of Tarxien and Ggantija. She .... (not see: *past perfect*) anything like that before.

Kevin and Fiona .... (be: *simple past*) very proud of the bargains they .... (get: *past perfect*) at the street market in Valetta. Kevin .... (buy: *past perfect*) some coins for his collection and Fiona .... (find: *past perfect*) a beautiful orange blouse there.

Übung 3 **Change the following sentences into the tense given in brackets.**

1. Kevin collected all sorts of coins. *(simple present)*

   ....

2. Mr Northam had forgotten to leave the key at the hotel reception. *(simple past)*

   ....

3. Mrs Northam enjoys looking at the beautiful sunset. *(past perfect)*

   ....

4. Fiona hadn't understood the language of the Maltese people. *(simple present)*

   ....

A 3. Zwei Kreuzworträtsel …
… und noch mehr unregelmäßige Verben

Übung 1

Fill in the English simple past forms.

ACROSS 2. blow, 5. come, 6. bring, 7. think, 9. begin, 10. bet, 13. hear, 14. shut, 15. sleep, 16. get, 18. fall, 20. swim, 22. throw, 23. spend, 24. feed, 26. lose, 28. find, 29. send, 30. meet

DOWN 1. understand, 2. buy, 3. break, 4. catch, 6. become, 8. go, 9. build, 11. write, 12. spell ,13. have, 14. speak ,17. beat, 19. leave, 20. stand, 21. eat, 23. shine, 25. drive, 27. sing

Übung 2 **Fill in the English past participles.**

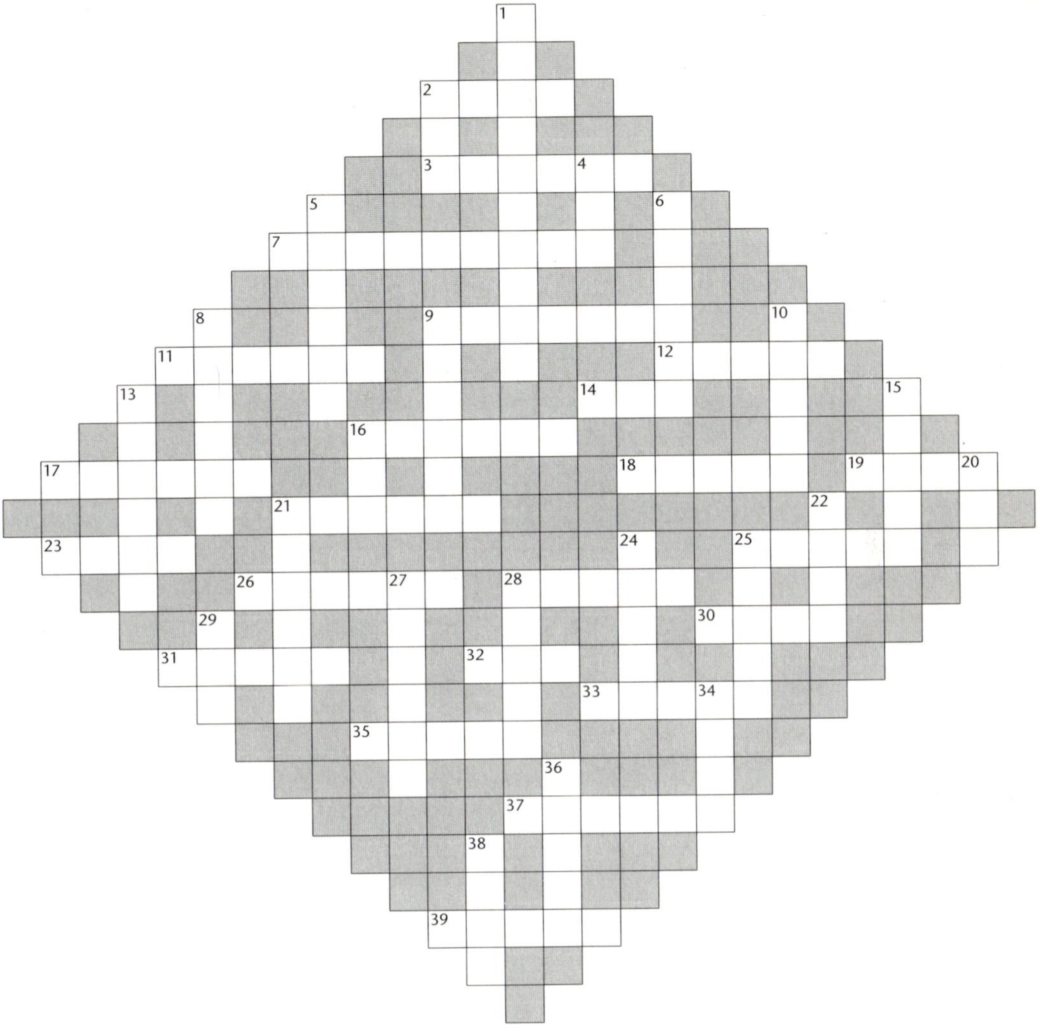

ACROSS 2. gemacht, 3. geworfen, 7. vergessen, 9. gebracht, 11. gefangen, 12. gegessen, 14. gelaufen, 16. gewählt, 17. gefroren, 18. gestanden, 19. gehalten, 21. gebissen, 23. geblutet, 25. geschlafen, 26. gekämpft, 28. gebaut, 30. zerrissen, 31. gegeben, 32. bekommen, 33. gewusst, 35. begonnen, 37. gefahren, 39. gefunden

DOWN 1. verstanden, 2. getroffen, 4. gewonnen, 5. gekauft, 6. geschlagen, 8. gefallen, 9. geworfen, 10. gehört, 13. gestohlen, 15. verbracht, 16. geschnitten, 20. gegraben, 21. gebrochen, 22. gewesen, 24. geflogen, 25. gezeigt, 27. versteckt, 28. geblasen, 29. geschlagen, 34. getragen (Kleidung), 36. gezeichnet, 38. erschossen

If-Sätze

1. If-Sätze: Grundtypen

Merke

Steht der **if-Satz am Anfang des Satzes, kann** er durch ein **Komma** vom Hauptsatz abgetrennt werden.
→ *If I practise every day, I will be able to juggle soon.*

Erscheint der **if-Satz nach dem Hauptsatz**, steht zwischen beiden Satzteilen kein Komma.
→ *I will be able to juggle soon if I practise every day.*

Grundtypen: Typ I
Die **Bedingung** im if-Satz wird für **erfüllbar** gehalten.
→ *If our team wins the match, we'll get new shirts.*
→ *We'll go camping if it doesn't rain.*
Bildung

if-Satz	Hauptsatz
Simple Present	will-Future

Grundtypen: Typ II
Die **Bedingung** wird für **nicht oder kaum erfüllbar** gehalten.
→ *If our team won the match, we'd get new shirts.*
→ *We'd go camping if it didn't rain.*
Bildung

if-Satz	Hauptsatz
Simple Past	*'d / would* + Infinitive (ohne *to*)

Im gesprochenen Englisch werden oft die Kurzformen ***'ll*** (statt ***will***) und ***'d*** (statt ***would***) verwendet.

Grundtypen: Typ III
Die **Bedingung** ist **nicht mehr erfüllbar**, weil sie sich auf die Vergangenheit bezieht.
→ *If our team had won the match, we would have got new shirts.*
→ *We'd have gone camping if it hadn't rained.*
Bildung

if-Satz	Hauptsatz
Past Perfect	*would have* + Past Participle

Merke

Im **if-Satz** darf **kein will-Future** und generell **kein *would*** stehen!

Übung 1 **Put the following sentences together.**

1. If my friend in Scotland had a computer …
2. Kevin would have come to Julia's birthday party in time …
3. If those cool trousers are still there tomorrow …
4. Vivian would go to the late show at the cinema …
5. If Jomo hadn't sprained his ankle …

◯ … I'll buy them.
◯ … if she didn't have a test tomorrow.
◯ … he would have taken part in the skateboard competition last weekend.
◯ … I would send her e-mails instead of ringing her every few days.
◯ … if his bike hadn't had a puncture.

Übung 2 **Write down whether the sentences from the previous exercise are conditional sentences of type I, type II or type III.**

	type
1. If my friend in Scotland had a computer, …	◯
2. Kevin would have come to Julia's birthday party in time …	◯
3. If those cool trousers are still there tomorrow, …	◯
4. Vivian would go to the late show at the cinema …	◯
5. If Jomo hadn't sprained his ankle, …	◯

Übung 3 **Kevin and some of his classmates are talking about holiday jobs. Fill in the missing verb forms.**

Type I:

1. If I work at the sports shop, I .... (get) a new pair of trainers at a cheaper price.
2. Alicia will get good tips if the manager of the golf club .... (employ) her as a waitress.

Type II:

3. If Pete .... (have) a motorbike, he would apply for a job at Safeway's supermarket. It's definitely too far to go by bike.
4. I would work at the take-away if they .... (pay) a little more!

Type III:

5. If Kevin hadn't broken his leg last summer, he .... (work) at the car wash.
6. I certainly wouldn't have minded the Sullivans' kids if I .... (know) that they never went to bed before eleven o'clock!

2. *If you need any help ...* If-Sätze – Typ I

Bei if-Sätzen des Typs I kann im Hauptsatz statt des **will-future** auch ***can, could, may, might, ought to, should, must*** oder ein **Imperativ** stehen.

→ *If the weather is all right,*	*we **may** / **might** / **can** / **could** **go** on a bike trip.*
→ *If you still have a temperature tomorrow,*	*you **ought to** / **should** / **must** **go** and see a doctor.*
→ *If you need any help,*	***don't hesitate**, just **call** me!*

Merke

Der if-Satz, der Hauptsatz oder auch beide Satzteile können verneint sein.

→ *If it **doesn't rain** tomorrow,*	*we can go roller-skating.*
→ *If it rains tomorrow,*	*we **won't be** able to go roller-skating.*
→ *If your cold **isn't** any better tomorrow,*	*you **shouldn't go** roller-skating.*

Übung 1

At the "Open Day" Samantha is talking to several pupils who want to go to Broughton High School next year.
Use the following auxiliaries to complete the sentences below.
must – will – don't – can – might – shouldn't

1. If you are interested in theatre and acting, you .... join the drama group.
2. If you are ill, you or your parents .... inform the school.
3. If you like music and dancing, you .... come to one of our school discos.
4. If your parents take you to school by car, they .... drive into the school grounds because there isn't much parking space there.
5. If you are keen on earrings, ... wear more than one in one ear! Nose or eye brow studs (*dt. (Ohr-)Stecker, hier: Piercing*) aren't allowed, either!
6. If you and your parents want to know more about the school, you .... find lots of interesting pieces of information in the "Broughton Bulletin" – that's our quarterly newsletter.

Übung 2

A group of eight pupils and teachers are organizing a "Fun & Sports Day".
Fill in the correct negative forms of the verbs in brackets.

1. If we don't find any sponsors, we .... (not have) any prizes for the song contest.
2. We could hold a skateboard competition if it .... (not rain).
3. If there .... (not be) any refreshments, the visitors won't stay long.
4. My uncle will lend us his stereo equipment if we .... (not let) anybody else get near it.
5. If we offer a number of different activities, people .... (not have) to queue up all the time.

Übung 3

Susanne, Vivian's penfriend from Germany, has invited Vivian to spend three weeks of her summer holidays in Germany.
Translate the missing parts of the following sentences into English.

1. Meine Schwester wird dir ihr Fahrrad leihen, wenn wir eine Fahrradtour machen wollen.

   ....

   .... *if we want to go on a bike trip.*

2. Wenn du Fahrradtouren nicht magst, können wir zum Schwimmen gehen.

   ....

   .... *, we can go swimming.*

3. Noch etwas: Wir werden in ein Open-Air-Konzert gehen, falls meine Freundin Karten bekommt.

   One other thing: We'll go to an open air concert ....

   ....

4. Wenn du genügend Platz im Koffer hast, bring deine Rollschuhe mit!

   If you've got enough space in your suitcase, ...

   ....

5. Wenn mein Vater keine Zeit hat, wird meine Mutter mit uns zu einem Freizeitpark fahren.

   ....

   .... *, Mum will go to a theme park with us.*

3. *If a fairy granted you one wish ...* If-Sätze – Typ II

Auch bei if-Sätzen des Typs II können im Hauptsatz statt ***would*** die Hilfsverben **might** oder **could** stehen.
→ *If we had a tennis teacher at our school, more pupils **could / might learn** to play tennis.*

Wenn sich jemand in die Lage einer anderen Person versetzt, verwendet man im if-Satz nach ***I, he, she*** oder ***it*** den Konjunktiv ***were.***
→ *Your swollen ankle doesn't look all too good. If I **were** you I would go and see a doctor.*

Merke

Auch bei den if-Sätzen des Typs II können der if-Satz, der Hauptsatz oder beide Satzteile verneint sein.

→ *If it **didn't rain**,*	*we might go roller-skating.*
→ *If the weather was nicer,*	*we **wouldn't sit** here.*
→ *If it **wasn't raining**,*	*we **wouldn't have** to stay inside.*

Übung 1

John Webster is a good tennis player. He has already won several tournaments.
Complete the following conditional sentences.

1. John wouldn't be so successful if he .... (not train) three or four times a week.
2. If John and Vivian had tickets for Wimbledon, they .... (watch) André Agassi live for the first time.
3. If the firm John's father works for .... (not sponsor) his son, John's sport would be too expensive for the Websters.
4. John would finish school even if he .... (earn) a lot of money as a professional tennis player.
5. His girlfriend Vivian .... (love) him even if he didn't win every match.

Übung 2

Jennifer has fallen in love with one of her brother's boyfriends but she doesn't know whether he likes her, too. Vivian and Sheila advise her what to do. Complete the sentences.

Vivian: If you .... (go) out with your brother and his boyfriend, and if your brother .... (pretend) to be tired and .... (go) home, "he" might give you a lift.

Sheila: If I .... (be) you, I .... (wear) that terrific blue top!

Jennifer: If I .... (not have) those braces, I .... (be) more self-confident.

Vivian: Honestly – if I .... (have) your looks, I .... (not worry) about braces!

Übung 3

Kevin and Sheila want to start a new section called "If a fairy granted you one wish ..." in the next school magazine. They made notes about people's answers. Now it will be your job to form sentences:

Chris (16): if / I / have / motorbike / it / not take hours / to get to school

....

....

Judy (14): if / we / not have / school in the afternoon / I / meet / my friends / more often.

....

....

Sarah (15): if / I / become / Hollywood star / I / have dinner / with Leonardo di Caprio.

....

....

Richard (15): if / I / win / free trip to the moon / I / send / my geography teacher / postcard

....

....

4. *If or when?*
Bedingung oder Zeitpunkt?

„*If*" in Konditionalsätzen (Bedingungssätzen) wird im Deutschen mit **„wenn, falls"** übersetzt.

→ ***If*** *I met Prince William, I would ask him about his hobbies.*

„When" steht in Temporalsätzen (Nebensätzen der Zeit) und wird mit **„wenn"** oder **„als"** wiedergegeben. Man benützt es für Ereignisse, die schon geschehen sind oder solche, die ganz sicher geschehen werden.

→ ***When*** *we were in Disneyland last year, I took a lot of photos.*

→ ***When*** *I'm older, I'll spend some time in Australia.*

Übung 1

Handelt es sich bei den fett gedruckten Satzteilen um Bedingungssätze oder um Nebensätze der Zeit?

	Bedingungs-satz	Nebensatz der Zeit
1. **Als Sheila eine Einladung von ihrer Tante aus Boston bekam,** war sie sehr aufgeregt.	○	○
2. Sie schrieb: „**Wenn du deine Eltern und deine Freunde nicht vermisst,** würde ich vorschlagen, dass du vier Wochen bleibst."	○	○
3. „**Wenn du ankommst,** hole ich dich vom Flughafen ab."	○	○
4. „Du kannst natürlich sofort deine Eltern anrufen, **wenn wir bei mir zu Hause sind.**"	○	○
5. **Wenn Sheilas Tante keinen Internetanschluss hätte,** könnte Sheilas Freund ihr keine E-Mails schicken.	○	○
6. **Wenn Sheila am Flughafen ist,** wird sie vor dem Abflug genügend Zeit haben einen Kaffee zu trinken.	○	○

Übung 2 **Now fill in *if* or *when*!**

1. .... Sheila got an invitation from her aunt in Boston, she was very excited.
2. She wrote: ".................... you don't miss your parents and your friends, I would suggest that you stay for four weeks."
3. ".................... you arrive, I will pick you up at the airport."
4. "Of course you can call your parents immediately .... we get to my place.
5. .... Sheila's aunt didn't have internet access, Sheila's boyfriend couldn't send her any e-mails.
6. .... Sheila is at the airport, she will have enough time for drinking a cup of coffee before the departure.

Übung 3 **Now it is your turn to translate!**

1. Chris ruft Sheila fast jeden Tag an, wenn sie von der Schule nach Hause kommt.

   ....

   ....

2. Als sie ihm von ihrer Reise nach Amerika erzählte, war er nicht sehr begeistert.

   ....

   ....

3. Chris fragte: „Wenn du in Boston einen netten Jungen kennen lernen würdest, würdest du dich in ihn verlieben?"

   ....

   ....

4. Sheilas Antwort: „Wenn du nicht aufhörst solche dummen Fragen zu stellen, schicke ich dir ein Foto von mir und Leonardo di Caprio!"

   ....

   ....

   ....

5. Chris lachte. „O.K.! Wenn ich vom Basketballtraining zurückkomme, hole ich dich ab und wir gehen ins Kino – ‚The Beach' mit Leonardo di Caprio läuft gerade!"

   ....

   ....

   ....

5. *Mixed exercises:* If-Sätze – Typ I und Typ II

Zur Erinnerung:

Beim **Typ I** wird die Bedingung für erfüllbar gehalten.
Im if-Satz steht das **Simple Present**, im Hauptsatz ***will, can, may, could*** **oder** ***might*** **+ Verb (Infinitiv).**

→ *If Kevin finds a good and inexpensive bike, he will buy it.*
→ *If it isn't raining, he might test it immediately.*

Beim **Typ II** wird die Bedingung für nicht oder kaum erfüllbar gehalten.
Im if-Satz steht das **Simple Past**, im Hauptsatz ***would, could*** **oder** ***might*** **+ Verb (Infinitiv).**

→ *If Sheila had better marks, her mother wouldn't worry so much.*
→ *If Sheila didn't go out every weekend, she would be unhappy.*

Übung 1

Kevin wants to buy some mountain bike equipment. His friend Jeremy gives him some tips.
Complete the following sentences. Choose from the box below.

1. If I were you,

2. If you want to buy a second-hand bike,

3. If you haven't got a helmet,

4. If I didn't have to study for that maths test,

5. If you intend to ride regularly,

… you should look for a good one that fits perfectly.

… I'd go to the bike shop with you.

… cycling shorts are a must. They have a padded insert *(dt. wattierte / gepolsterte Einlage)* and make cycling much more comfortable.

… check the main mountain bike magazines for classified ads *(dt. Kleinanzeigen).*

… I'd join a cycling club. That's great fun and you can learn a lot!

Übung 2

Sheila wants to go out in the evening, but her mother doesn't like the idea at all.
Fill in the correct verb forms.

Sheila: If you .... (allow) me to go out tonight, I .... (be) back at midnight, I promise.

Mrs Ragunathan: If you .... (not go) out so often, you could have much better marks at school.

Sheila: But Mum! If I only stayed at home, life .... (be) terribly boring and I .... (not study) more than I do now! I promise – if you let me go out tonight, I .... (not go) out tomorrow.

Mrs Ragunathan: If you .... (show) just a little more enthusiasm for your school subjects, I wouldn't have anything to worry about.

Sheila: If Sheila Ragunathan .... (not get) an A or a B in her next test, she won't go out for a whole month. Is that a deal?

Mrs Ragunathan: That sounds fine.

Übung 3

It's Friday evening. Chris, John, Alison and Sheila want to go out together. Complete the following conditional sentences.

1. John: If somebody has got today's newspaper, we .... (have) a look what's on at the cinema.
2. Alison: If the new James Bond film is on, ... (not count) me in! I hate James Bond!
3. Chris: If we .... (live) in London, we would be able to go to the fairground at the Millennium Dome.
4. Sheila: The Escape Club would be a nice place to go to if they .... (not play) such terrible music!
5. Alison: If you .... (be) hungry, we can have a snack first. There's a new Italian pasta bar in Lancaster Road.
6. Sheila: I can only go there if somebody .... (lend) me five pounds.
7. John: O.K. – if we all hurry up, we .... (catch) the bus!

6. *If things had been different ...* If-Sätze – Typ III

If-Sätze des Typs III beziehen sich immer auf die **Vergangenheit**.

Im if-Satz steht das **Past Perfect,** im Hauptsatz sind die folgenden Varianten möglich:

→ *If the school team **had lost** the match, everybody **would have been** disappointed.*

→ *If Alison **had left** earlier, she **might have caught** the train.*

→ *If John **had brought** his camera, he **could have taken** some pictures.*

Merke

Auch beim Typ III können der if-Satz, der Hauptsatz oder beide Satzteile verneint sein.

→ *If there **hadn't been** such a strong wind, John would have come by motorbike.*

→ *If it had rained, John **wouldn't have come** by motorbike.*

→ *If the weather **hadn't been** so good, John **wouldn't have come** by motorbike.*

Übung 1

If things had been different in some films, many cinemagoers would have been surprised!
Complete the following conditional sentences.

1. If Anakin Skywalker .... (be) a girl in "Star Wars: Episode I", she would have been the first female Jedi knight.
2. Fewer hankies would have become soaked with tears if Leonardo di Caprio .... (survive) in "Titanic".
3. If Shakespeare hadn't fallen in love, his career as a playwright .... (come) to a quick end.
4. Mr Bean's American host family .... (not protest) if he had moved out of their house.
5. If Arnold Schwarzenegger .... (not show) his muscles in his latest film, it might have become a flop.
6. Julia Roberts .... (not fall) in love with Hugh Grant in *Notting Hill* if he hadn't spilled his orange juice on her T-shirt.
7. If Rhett Butler .... (not look) so handsome, Scarlett O'Hara mightn't have fallen for him. (she has fallen for him, *dt. er hat es ihr angetan*)

Übung 2

It was one of those days for Kevin. Everything that could go wrong went wrong. Complete what Kevin told his classmates the following day.

Kevin listened to the sports news on the radio. That's why he missed the bus. So he got his motorbike out of the garden-shed. Unfortunately he tore his new jacket. He was so furious that he kicked his motorbike. The motorbike fell on his foot. He played badly at the football match. His team lost the match.

"Yesterday wasn't my lucky day! If I hadn't listened to the sports news on the radio, I wouldn't have missed the bus. If I .... the bus, I ....

....

....

....

....

....

....

....

....

Übung 3

John didn't do well in his last maths test. What could he have done better? Translate into English.

Wenn John besser gelernt hätte, hätte er nicht so viele Fehler gemacht.

.... he wouldn't have made so many mistakes.

Wenn er nicht die ganze Nacht gefeiert hätte, hätte er einen klaren Kopf behalten.

If he had not been partying all night, ...

....

Wenn er seine Armbanduhr nicht vergessen hätte, wäre ihm die Zeit nicht davon gelaufen.

....

...., time wouldn't have run out for him.

Johns Vater hätte mit ihm gelernt, wenn er ihn gefragt hätte.

....

.... if he had asked him.

7. Mixed exercises – Typ I, II und III

Zur Erinnerung noch einmal alle drei Typen von if-Sätzen im Überblick:

Typ I: → *If John **catches** a fish, he **will throw** it back into the water.*

Typ II: → *If John **caught** a fish, he **would throw** it back into the water.*

Typ III: → *If John **had caught** a fish, he **would have thrown** it back into the water.*

Die verneinten Formen findest du auf den Seiten 14, 16 und 22.

Übung 1

John's father is an enthusiastic angler. He and his son often go fishing together.

1. Even if John and his father didn't catch any fish, ...

....

2. They will go on a fishing holiday next summer ....

....

3. They would have gone last spring ....

....

4. If John didn't have to be out at the crack of dawn *(dt. in aller Frühe)*, ...

....

5. If they had a boat, ...

....

6. John's father wouldn't have become soaking wet last weekend ....

....

Choose from the list below to complete the sentences.

... he would enjoy their fishing trips even more.
... if he hadn't slipped and fallen into the water.
... they would have a lot of fun together.
... they could go out onto the river and fish in different areas.
... if John hadn't caught a bad cold.
... if it doesn't cost a fortune.

Übung 2 **One type of if-sentence is given in this exercise. Add the two missing types.**

Type I: John's father can't go fishing with his son in the holidays if he doesn't get a day off from work.

Type II: ....

....

Type III: ....

....

Type I: ....

....

Type II: If Fiona found a well-paid summer job, she would buy a new stereo.

Type III: ....

....

Type I: ....

....

Type II: ....

....

Type III: John would have brought us some pizzas if the take-away round the corner had been open.

Type I: If it doesn't rain, the Hendersons will go camping.

Type II: ....

....

Type III: ....

....

Übung 3 **Complete the following jokes by using the correct form of the verbs in brackets.**

On the top of a high mountain in the Austrian Alps there is a sign warning climbers: "Be careful not to fall. It's a dangerous place. But if you .... (fall), look to the right. The Alps are beautiful!"

A young lady is standing in front of her wardrobe complaining to her husband: "Just look at my clothes. If anyone .... (come), they might think I was a cook. Her husband replies calmly: "If they .... (stay) for dinner they wouldn't!"

8. More mixed exercises – Typ I, II und III

Merke

Neben den **Bedingungssätzen des Typs I, II und III** gibt es – wie im Deutschen – **Mischformen**. Der Satz muss einen logischen Sinn ergeben.

→ *If Jeremy hadn't fallen off his bike, his trousers wouldn't be dirty.*

→ *If he wasn't a good cyclist, he wouldn't have won so many prizes.*

Übung 1

UKkids online is Samantha's favourite web site. There she can find a lot of information about her favourite pop stars.
Fill in the correct forms of the verbs in brackets.

If Britney Spears hadn't been such a talented girl, she .... (not become) a TV star at 11. Her music videos wouldn't have earned so much praise if she .... (not take) dance classes for years. If her single and album sales continue to break records, she .... (become) a big star. Robbie Williams would be an actor now if he .... (not respond) to the newspaper ad of a band some years ago. If Robbie hadn't drunk too much, he .... (not dive) into the fountain of a hotel and he .... (not have) a scar just above his eyes now.

Übung 2

Jeremy is a very successful mountain biker.
Choose from the following list of verbs to complete the text.
Put the verbs in the correct form.
hurt – train – not have – sponsor – not join – visit

If Jeremy .... the local cycling club two years ago, he wouldn't be so good at this sport now. If he .... hard, he can win the cross-country course next month. And if Jeremy wins the competition, a local helmet manufacturer .... him for two years.

Jeremy and his friends usually ride in the Forest Enterprise woodlands where there are marked trails for cyclists. If they .... good cycling equipment, their parents wouldn't let them do this sport. Last year Jeremy fell off his bike and .... himself badly if he hadn't had such a good helmet. When Jeremy .... his cousin Greg next weekend, Greg will show him the most exciting trails in the area.

Übung 3

Vivian O'Brian would like to work as an au pair after finishing school. Here are parts of the conversation between Vivian and her friend Sharon.
Fill in the correct verb forms.

Sharon: I heard that you can be an au pair if you .... (be) between 18 and 30 years old – is that right?

Vivian: Yes, that's true. And you don't have to be a girl! If I .... (have) enough money, I would go to the United States for a holiday. But if I work as an au pair, I .... (get) pocket money and I .... (not have to pay) anything for room and board.

Sharon: Can you switch families if you .... (not get along) with your host family?

Vivian: Yes, you can. Your au pair agency will help you. That's why it's important to find an agency that belongs to an international au pair organization.

By the way – if I .... (not have) any childcare experience, I wouldn't be accepted by some agencies.

Sharon: If my sister's friend had gathered more information about being an au pair, I'm sure she .... (not have) such a negative experience.

Vivian: If I like the States, maybe I .... (stay) there!

Sharon: If I .... (not have) such a fear of flying, I would come with you.

Übung 4

Translate into English what a former au pair says about her year in the USA.

1. Wenn du Kinder und Hausarbeit nicht magst, solltest du nicht als Au Pair arbeiten.

....

....

2. Viele Au Pairs wären nicht so überrascht, wenn sie ihre Gastfamilie sorgfältiger ausgewählt hätten.

....

....

3. Wenn ich unter 21 gewesen wäre, wäre es für mich in den USA viel schwieriger gewesen am Abend auszugehen.

....

....

B 9. *If only …* – Irreale Wunschsätze

Mit ***if only …*** und **Past Tense** oder mit ***I wish …*** und **Past Tense** bringst du dein Bedauern darüber zum Ausdruck, dass etwas nicht so ist, wie du es gerne hättest.

→ ***If only** I **had** a better mark in the English test.*

→ ***I wish** I **had** a better mark in the English test.*

Die verneinte Form wird so gebildet:

→ ***If only** I **didn't have** so much homework.*

→ ***I wish** I **didn't have** so much homework.*

Beim **Verb *be*** steht in der **1. und 3. Person Singular** nach ***if only …*** und ***I wish …*** die Form ***were***:

→ *I wish I **were** a little taller.*

→ *If only our neighbour **weren't** so unfriendly.*

Die Form ***was*** wird nur in der Umgangssprache verwendet.

Bedauerst du, dass etwas in der **Vergangenheit** nicht so verlaufen ist, wie es hätte verlaufen sollen, so verwendest du nach ***if only …*** und ***I wish …*** das **Past Perfect**.

→ *If only I **had cycled** a little more slowly.*

→ *I wish I **hadn't eaten** so much cake.*

Übung 1

Vivian is ill. She is lying in bed with flu.
Fill in the correct simple past forms.

1. I wish I .... (not have) a temperature.
2. If only my throat .... (not hurt) so much.
3. I wish Sheila .... (be) here.
4. Wasn't that the doorbell? If only someone .... (come) to visit me.
5. I wish I .... (feel) better. I can't even read a book.
6. If only the hours .... (pass) a little more quickly.
7. If only those church bells .... (not ring) every quarter of an hour.

Übung 2

Samantha celebrated her birthday yesterday. She had invited lots of friends. Now she is thinking about the party.
Fill in the correct past perfect forms of the verbs.

1. If only I .... (make) more sandwiches.
2. I wish Pete .... (not talk) so much.
3. If only Jomo .... (not drop) a full bottle of coke.
4. I wish Susan .... (play) a few songs on the guitar.
5. If only I .... (ask) Karen to bring some of her CDs.
6. I wish Steve .... (compliment) me on my new dress.

Übung 3

Kevin and some of his classmates went camping for three days. On the second day it started to rain and did not stop for hours. Put together what the friends were saying while they were sitting in their tent. Use the correct forms of the verbs.

Alison: If only / the rain / stop .

....

Roger: I wish / we / pack / our raincoats .

....

Kevin: If only / we / watch / the weather forecast .

....

Sheila: I wish / I / not have / wet feet .

....

Jomo: If only / I / find / my cards . Then / we / can play / a game of rummy *(dt. Rommé)*.

....

....

John: I wish / you / not complain / about everything .

....

B

10. *Had it stopped raining …* Verdrehte Bedingungssätze

Should kann im if-Satz stehen, wenn es sich um eine **denkbare Möglichkeit** handelt. Im Hauptsatz steht der Imperativ, *will* + Verb oder *would* + Verb.

→ *If we should come to the cinema late, please buy tickets for us, too.*
→ *If we should miss the bus, we'll take the next one.*
→ *If we should miss the bus, we might ask Dad to give us a lift.*

Wie im Deutschen kann ein solcher Bedingungssatz umgestellt werden:

→ ***If we should come** later, we'll give you a ring.*
Wenn wir später kommen sollten, rufen wir dich an.
→ ***Should we come** later, we'll give you a ring.*
Sollten wir später kommen, rufen wir dich an.

Auch Bedingungssätze des Typs III können auf diese Weise umgestellt werden. Sie klingen dann etwas förmlicher.

→ ***Had Gregory paid** attention, he would know the answer.*
(If Gregory had paid attention, …)
→ ***Had Sandra not left** her window open, her room would not have been flooded.*
(If Sandra had not left her window open, …)

Übung 1

Jomo is reading the instruction sheet of his VCR (video cassette recorder). Change the sentences, using *if*.

1. Should you want to watch a bilingual programme, you can select the language.

....

...., you can select the language.

2. Should the remote control unit *(dt. Fernbedienung)* not operate, change the batteries.

....

...., change the batteries.

3. Should there be any recording trouble, the clock time might not be set correctly.

....

...., the clock time might not be set correctly.

4. Should the sound quality be poor, the tape might be defective.

....

...., the tape might be defective.

Übung 2

There was an article in the newspaper about an 11-year-old boy who had been blown over a 250 feet cliff and had survived. John, his sister and his parents are talking about the boy's lucky escape. Change the sentences – don't use *if*.

Mr Webster: If the boy's father hadn't gone for a walk with his son in such stormy weather, this wouldn't have happened.

....

with his son in such stormy weather, this wouldn't have happened.

Mrs Webster: If they hadn't walked so close to the edge of the cliff, it wouldn't have been so dangerous.

....

...., it wouldn't have been so dangerous.

John: If the boy had fallen into the water, he might have drowned.

....

...., he might have drowned.

Mrs Webster: If it had taken longer to call for help, the boy might have died.

....

...., the boy might have died.

Sarah: If the RAF (= Royal Air Force) helicopter crew hadn't been so excellent, they might not have been able to rescue the boy from the bottom of the cliffs.

....

...., they might not have been able to rescue the boy from the bottom of the cliffs.

Übung 3

Jomo got a new skateboard for his birthday. Of course he wanted to try it out immediately. Unfortunately he fell and broke his wrist. Translate the following sentences into English.

1. Hätte er mit dem neuen Skateboard etwas länger geübt, wäre das nicht passiert.

....

2. Wäre er nicht in die Luft gesprungen, wäre er nicht hingefallen.

....

3. Sollte er versuchen, mit seinem gebrochenen Arm zu fahren, würde seine Mutter sein Skateboard verstecken.

....

....

C Futurformen

1. Spontane Absichtserklärung: will-Future

Hat man gerade im Moment des Sprechens einen Entschluss gefasst, verwendet man das **will-Future.**
Im Deutschen steht in diesen Fällen in der Regel das Präsens.
→ *It's pretty hot today. **I'll buy** an ice-cream.*
Es ist ziemlich heiß heute. Ich kaufe mir (jetzt) ein Eis.
→ *That's the phone. **I'll answer** it.*
Das ist das Telefon. Ich gehe ran.

Die verneinte Form lautet: *won't (will not)* + Verb (Infinitiv)
→ *Look, it has stopped raining. I **won't take** an umbrella.*

Man verwendet häufig ***I think I'll…*** und ***I don't think I'll…***.
→ *I'm not very hungry. **I think I'll** just **have** a sandwich for dinner.*
→ *I don't feel very well. **I don't think I'll go** to the party.*
*(or: **I think I won't go** to the party.)*

Übung 1

**Jomo and John go to Manchester to watch a football match.
What do they say in the following situations?
Form complete English sentences.**

1. After Jomo and John have got off the train in Manchester, they want to get a city map.
   John: I / go / to the information desk / over there

   ....

2. They don't know from which platform the train back home will leave in the evening.
   Jomo: I / have a look / at the timetable

   ....

3. In front of the stadium there is a stand where fan articles are sold.
   John: I / think / I / buy / one of those T-shirts

   ....

   Jomo: I / not think / I / get / one. – Look at the price – they are 10 pounds each!

   ....

4. John wants to get something to drink.
   John: I / be / right back

   ....

Übung 2

**In the following situations you decide to do (or not to do) something at the time of speaking.
Write down what you will or won't do.**

1. Your friend has borrowed some books from the library. Now she is ill and you promise to return the books for her. ....

2. You have a toothache. You decide to go to the dentist's. I think ....

3. You wanted to invite 20 guests to your birthday party. But now you have changed your mind. ....

4. There's a new film on at the cinema. You decide to ring and ask your friend Robert if he wants to come along. ....

5. You have ridden on a roller coaster and now you don't feel too well. You decide not to ride again. ....

Übung 3

**Kevin, Sheila and their friends have taken part in the volleyball tournament at Broughton High. Now they are exhausted.
Translate what they decide to do.**

1. John: Das erste, was ich jetzt tue – ich dusche.

   ....

2. Kevin: Ich hänge unsere Urkunde im Klassenzimmer auf. (Urkunde, *engl. certificate)*

   ....

3. Samantha: Ich glaube, ich esse drei Portionen Spaghetti.

   ....

4. Sheila: Ich glaube nicht, dass ich heute noch mal einen Ball anfasse.

   ....

5. Jomo: Ich gehe heim und schaue mir das *Star Wars* Video an.

   ....

6. Vivian: Ich lege Eis auf meinen Daumen. Er ist ganz schön angeschwollen.

   ....

2. Geplantes Vorhaben: going-to-Future

Bei Vorhaben bzw. Entscheidungen, die schon länger feststehen, d. h. nicht gerade erst spontan gefasst wurden, verwendet man das **going-to-Future**.

→ *John **is going to visit** his cousin in the holidays.*

→ *I'm **going to repair** my bike this afternoon.*

Bildung:

bejahter Satz

am / are / is + *going to* + Verb (Infinitiv)

verneinter Satz

am / are / is + *not* + *going to* + Verb (Infinitiv)

Häufig werden die Kurzformen *I'm going to, he's going to, we aren't going to* etc. verwendet.

Übung 1

What are the families in Hill Street going to do at the weekend? Read the clues and complete the table.

10	12	14	16
The Taylors	....	....	....
are going to	are going to	are going to	are going to
....	....	....	....
....	....	....	....

1. The family who is going to buy a new computer lives in number 16.
2. The Hendersons live next to the Taylors.
3. The Hendersons' other neighbours, the O'Sullivans, are going to visit friends in York.
4. The people who are going to have a barbecue party do not live next to the O'Sullivans.
5. The Campbells are not going to visit friends and they are not going to have a barbecue party.
6. Which family is going to paint their kitchen?

Übung 2

What are the pupils of Broughton High School going to do in the summer holidays?
Form complete English sentences.

1. Alison: work at Safeway's supermarket

....

2. Greg + Laura: go to an open-air concert

....

3. Steve: take part in a kite festival in Coventry

....

4. Gloria: attend a language course in France

....

5. Patrick: spend two weeks in a summer camp in Wales

....

Übung 3

Vanessa didn't do very well in the last German test. Now she has a lot of good intentions.
Translate into English.

1. Ich fange nicht am letzten Tag vor der Prüfung mit dem Lernen an.

....

....

2. Ich lerne jeden Tag eine Viertelstunde lang Wörter.

....

....

3. Ich kaufe ein Buch mit Übungen und mache jedes Wochenende ein paar Aufgaben.

....

....

4. Am Samstag schlafe ich nicht bis 11 Uhr, sondern stehe um 8 Uhr auf.

....

....

5. Ich gebe meiner Deutschlehrerin jede Woche einen Aufsatz zum Korrigieren.

....

....

3. Allgemeine Vorhersage oder Vermutung: will-Future

Im Englischen verwendet man das **will-Future** auch, wenn man eine Vorhersage machen will. Diese kann sich auf das Wetter, auf die Zukunft von Personen oder auf allgemeine Begebenheiten beziehen. Im Deutschen steht in diesen Fällen häufig das Präsens.

→ *In a week's time **we'll be** in Spain.*
In einer Woche sind wir schon in Spanien.

→ *Don't worry. You'**ll get** the job.*
Mach dir keine Sorgen. Du bekommst den Job.

Oft steht das will-Future nach Ausdrücken wie diesen:

→ *I expect*	ich erwarte, denke
→ *I'm sure*	ich bin sicher
→ *I hope*	ich hoffe
→ *probably*	wahrscheinlich

Übung 1

Peter and his girlfriend Claire are planning to make a trip to Edinburgh at the weekend, but only if the weather is fine. Complete the weather forecast for Scotland.
Use the following verbs:
bring – be – come – not find – fall – be – calm – rise – blow – need

1. Tomorrow there .... some heavy rain showers in the north of Scotland. The temperature .... below 8°C and you .... warm clothes.
2. Strong winds .... from the east. They .... away the clouds in the late afternoon.
3. The sun .... any clouds to hide behind on Saturday. The winds .... down and the temperature .... to 18°C.
4. Sunday .... excellent weather for all kinds of outdoor activities. It .... sunny and warm all day with temperatures rising to 22°C.

Übung 2

**Claire's best friend, Conny, is sure that Claire and Peter will enjoy their trip to Edinburgh.
Form complete English sentences.**

1. I'm sure / you / be impressed / by the castle.

2. you / probably / taste a whisky / at the Scotch Whisky Heritage Centre

3. I expect / you / spend / some time / at the waterfront

4. I'm sure / you / try out / lots of / excellent restaurants, bistros and pubs

5. I expect / you / visit / *The Tavern* / the oldest pub in Scotland

6. I hope / you / have / lots of fun

Übung 3

**In your horoscope you can read wonderful things about your future.
Translate into English.**

1. Nächste Woche wirst du von einem lieben Freund überrascht.

2. Das kommende Wochenende wird sehr aufregend für dich.

3. Du bekommst einen Brief, der dein Leben verändern wird.

4. Zwischen dem 14. und dem 18. triffst du einen alten Freund.

5. Dein Traumpartner wird in dein Leben treten, aber du siehst ihn nicht gleich.

6. Im Sommer wird sich einer deiner Träume erfüllen.

7. Dein Geldbeutel wird nicht lange leer bleiben.

4. Es bahnt sich etwas an: going-to-Future

Das **going-to-Future** wird dann verwendet, wenn aufgrund **deutlicher Anzeichen** bereits erkennbar ist, dass sich etwas ereignen wird. Meist bezieht sich das Gesagte auf die nahe Zukunft.
Auch in diesen Fällen steht im Deutschen häufig das Präsens.

→ *Look at those dark clouds. It's **going to rain** soon.*
... Es fängt bald an zu regnen.

→ *She's so furious. She's **going to slap** his face.*
... Sie gibt ihm gleich eine Ohrfeige.

Übung 1

What's going to happen? Choose from the list below and connect the sentences that belong together.

1. Vivian feels terrible.
2. Look at James Bond's sports car!
3. Take an umbrella with you.
4. Today there is more traffic in the streets than usual.
5. Those football players look very tired.
6. There was an accident in Preston Road.
7. Don't park your car here.
8. John is running round the corner.

... It's going to explode in a second.
... The ambulance is going to arrive soon.
... You are going to get a ticket.
... She thinks she's going to be sick.
... He's going to catch the bus.
... It's going to rain soon.
... I think I'm going to be late for work.
... The other team is going to score a goal any minute.

Übung 2

Claire and Peter are in Edinburgh. They are walking along the waterfront at Leith, Edinburgh's port.
Complete the sentences with *going to*, using the verbs in brackets.

Claire: There are so many nice places around here. This .... (be) a really trendy area.

Peter: Don't walk so close to the edge of the pier. You .... (fall) into the water!

Claire: And you .... (rescue) me, aren't you?

Peter: How about having lunch instead? I'm hungry – and I .... (not look) at another seafood restaurant without going in.

Übung 3

In the afternoon Claire and Peter go to the city centre.
Complete the sentences with *going to*, using the verbs in brackets.

Claire: Why didn't you take your jacket. You .... (feel) cold pretty soon.

Peter: No, I'm not. I .... (sit) very close to you.

Claire: Look, the sale is on at the moment. They .... (have) fantastic prices in the shops.

Peter: That's a nice blouse. It .... (look) terrific on you! But maybe I should get a jacket …

Übung 4

Claire and Peter are watching a thriller at the cinema. What's going to happen in the following scenes?
Translate into English.

1. A man is running towards the edge of a cliff. — Ein Hubschrauber kommt gleich und rettet ihn.
....
2. The lights go out. — Gleich hören wir einen fürchterlichen Schrei.
....
3. A woman in a sports car is driving too fast. — Das Auto wird sich gleich überschlagen.
....
4. The police detective is looking into the woman's eyes. — Sie werden sich ineinander verlieben.
....

5. Will-Future oder going-to-Future?

Hier noch einmal die wichtigsten Aspekte im Überblick:

Plan, Vorhaben, Absicht:

will-Future bei spontanen Entschlüssen, die erst während des Sprechens gefasst werden

→ *I'm very busy at the moment, but I'll ring you back in the evening.*

going-to-Future bei Vorhaben und Entscheidungen, die schon länger feststehen

→ *We are going to meet some friends at the pub tonight.*

Vorhersage:

will-Future bei allgemeinen Vorhersagen und Vermutungen

→ *You'll have a wonderful time in New York!*

going-to-Future wenn deutliche Anzeichen bereits erkennen lassen, dass sich etwas ereignen wird

→ *We are going to land in a few minutes.*

Übung 1

Samantha and Sheila go to a street market. Put the verbs in brackets into the right form, using *will* or *going to*.

Samantha: I .... (visit) my German penfriend in August. Maybe I'll find a nice present for her.

Sheila: You .... (speak) German fluently when you come back. Look, they sell power bead bracelets *(dt. Perlenarmbänder)* over there.

I .... (get) a pink one for myself – that's for love and romance.

Samantha: That's a nice cardigan. I .... (try) it on.

Sheila: Give me your bag. I .... (hold) it for you. Be careful – that pile of T-shirts .... (fall).

Samantha: What .... you .... (wear) at Jill's birthday next week?

Sheila: I don't know yet. I hope I .... (find) something nice here on the market.

Übung 2

Jomo and John are talking about computer technology. Put the sentences together.

1. I'm going to do
2. Do you think
3. Why don't we start our own Internet business?
4. My dad is going to contact
5. I'm pretty sure
6. There will be a growing demand

- ◯ a business partner in California.
- ◯ I'm sure we'll make a lot of money.
- ◯ for web designers in the future.
- ◯ a course in computer programming.
- ◯ he'll offer me a holiday job.
- ◯ I'll be able to make my own Internet homepage soon?

Übung 3

A class at Broughton High School wants to organize a "Nature Day". This is what they plan to do. Put the verbs in brackets into the right form, using *will* or *going to*.

Jeff: Kevin and I have already decided what we ………………………… (do). Kevin ………………………… (send) an e-mail to the World Land Trust and ask for material. I ………………………… (collect) articles about the rainforest in Brazil.

Jennifer: I'm sure people ………………………… (want) to get information about environmental projects in Britain, too.

Eve: That's a good idea. My uncle is a ranger. I ………………………… (phone) him and interview him about his job. I expect he ………………………… (know) about projects in the area.

Oliver: I've collected some walkabout leaflets for discovering the local countryside. I ………………………… (cut) out the pictures and maps and make a poster.

Jennifer: By the way – Ms Leigh ………………………… (let) us use some geography lessons for preparing the project.

6. Das Simple Present bei Fahrplänen und Öffnungszeiten

Das **Simple Present** – die einfache Form der Gegenwart – kommt immer dann zum Einsatz, wenn über **zukünftige Ereignisse** gesprochen wird, **die von offiziellen Stellen oder anderen Personen festgelegt wurden**, z. B.:
- Fahr- und Flugpläne
- Geburtstage, Feiertage
- Öffnungszeiten
- Veranstaltungstermine

Im Deutschen wird ebenfalls das Präsens verwendet.

→ *My train leaves in half an hour.*
Mein Zug fährt in einer halben Stunde.

→ *What time does the museum open tomorrow?*
Um welche Zeit öffnet morgen das Museum?

→ *Next Saturday the performance doesn't start at 8 o'clock, but half an hour earlier.*
Am kommenden Samstag fängt die Vorstellung nicht um 8 Uhr an, sondern eine halbe Stunde früher.

Übung 1

The Northams are going to fly to San Francisco next week. Translate into English.

1. Das Flugzeug fliegt um 6 Uhr morgens ab.

2. Wir müssen nicht umsteigen, es ist ein Direktflug.

3. Der Flug dauert 13 Stunden.

4. Wir kommen um ungefähr 10 Uhr Ortszeit im Hotel an.

5. Der erste Tag unseres Aufenthalts ist in den USA ein Feiertag.

6. Es ist schade, dass das Theaterfestival nicht eine Woche früher anfängt.

Übung 2

Tom is in London for the first time and he has a lot of questions. Find the correct verbs and forms of *to do* and complete the sentences.
arrive – start – leave – close – open – go

1. When .... the Tate Gallery .... tomorrow morning?
2. .... the sightseeing buses .... every hour this afternoon?
3. .... the 11.15 train to Windsor .... from Victoria station?
4. When .... the train .... at Windsor?
5. What time .... the football match Arsenal vs. Leeds ....?
6. When .... the big department stores .... tonight?

Übung 3

Susanne worked out an interview with Harry Potter, the young magician, for the school magazine.
Translate the sentences into English.

Susanne: Harry, wann sind deine Sommerferien zu Ende?
Harry: Am 1. September fängt die Schule wieder an – und ich freue mich schon darauf.
Susanne: Wie kommst du zurück nach Hogwarts Castle? Mit Zauberkraft? (Zauberkraft , *engl. magic power*)
Harry: Nein, mit dem Zug. Der Hogwarts Express fährt um 11 Uhr von Gleis neun-dreiviertel ab und kommt am Abend in Hogwarts Castle an.
Susanne: Dürft ihr am ersten Abend länger aufbleiben?
Harry: Nein, um 23 Uhr wird das Licht ausgeschaltet.

Susanne: ....

....

Harry: ....

....

Susanne: ....

....

Harry: ....

....

....

Susanne: ....

....

Harry: ....

....

7. Feste Vereinbarung: Present Progressive

Das **Present Progressive** kann in bestimmten Fällen auf zukünftige Ereignisse hinweisen. Es handelt sich dabei um **vorher getroffene Vereinbarungen** bzw. **festgelegte Termine**.
Meist wird durch eine Zeitangabe deutlich, dass es sich um die Zukunft und nicht um die Gegenwart handelt.
→ *What **are** you **doing** on Friday evening?*
→ *I'**m going** to the cinema.*
Anstelle des **Present Progressive** ist häufig auch das **going-to-Future** möglich.

Übung 1

This is Jomo's diary for next week. Form sentences, using the progressive form.

Sun	2 p.m.	play golf with Gerald and Steve
Mon	3 p.m.	meet Vivian in town
Tue	6 p.m.	watch football match
Wed	2.30 p.m.	dentist's
Thu	4 p.m.	driving lesson
Fri	7 p.m.	help John repair his motorbike

1. Jomo is playing golf with Gerald and Steve on Sunday afternoon.
2. ......
3. ......
4. ......
5. ......
6. ......

Übung 2

Fiona is telling her friend Vivian about her family's holiday plans. Form complete sentences, use the progressive form.

1. Mum, Dad and I / fly / to Majorca / in August.

....

2. My brother Jim / not come / with us.

....

3. He / go camping / in Wales / with some friends.

....

4. Some friends of ours / join / us / in the second week.

....

5. What / you / do / in the summer holidays?

....

Übung 3

Some people are making arrangements or getting information. Put the verbs into the simple or progressive present.

1. Mrs O'Brien: Vivian, the Tylers .... (have) a barbecue party next Saturday. Would you like to come along?

   Vivian: Yes, I'd love to. What time .... it .... (start)?

2. Geena: Hi, Steve. Jack and I .... (play) crazy golf this afternoon. .... you .... (come) with us?

   Steve: Sorry, I .... (help) Brian paint his room.

3. Samantha: Dad, we .... (go) on an excursion on Tuesday. Could you give me and Sheila a lift to the station? The train .... (leave) at 7.30 a.m.

   Mr Henderson: OK. Tell Sheila that we .... (pick) her up at 7.

4. Kevin: What time .... school .... (start) tomorrow?

   Jomo: It .... (start) at 9.45.

5. Announcement: Due to reconstruction work in progress the 9.30 train to Manchester .... (leave) from platform 3 today, but from platform 8.

8. Nebensätze mit *if, when, as soon as, before, until* und *while*

Wenn der Hauptsatz bereits zum Ausdruck bringt, dass es sich um Zukünftiges handelt, steht in Nebensätzen mit *if, when, after, as soon as, before, until* und *while* das **Simple Present** (die einfache Form der Gegenwart).

→ **If** you **go** now, I'll never look at you again.
→ What are you going to be **when** you **leave** school in two years' time?
→ I'll be leaving **as soon as** Mum **comes** back.
→ Don't forget to brush your teeth **before** you **go** to bed.
→ I'm afraid, Debby has to wait **until** the bank **opens**.
→ I'd really love to look after your baby **while** you'**re** at the party.

Übung 1 **Complete the sentences by choosing a) or b).**

1. I'll come to see you
   ◯ a) till you come back.
   ◯ b) before you leave.

2. I can't wait
   ◯ a) till he comes.
   ◯ b) as soon as he rings me up.

3. Mr Jackson will complain about his neighbour's dog
   ◯ a) when it stops barking.
   ◯ b) if it doesn't stop barking.

4. Mrs Burnes will be very angry
   ◯ a) when she sees that her children have smashed her favourite flower pot.
   ◯ b) before her children tell her about the damage they have done.

5. As soon as we go to bed
   ◯ a) there will be this strange noise coming from the attic.
   ◯ b) we are going to have dinner.

6. We'll have to stay up
   ◯ a) when the shops open in the morning.
   ◯ b) until the last guest leaves the house.

7. I'll let you know
   ◯ a) as soon as I hear from my boy-friend.
   ◯ b) until I hear from my boyfriend.

8. Don't say anything
   ◯ a) as soon as you know the whole story.
   ◯ b) before you know the whole story.

9. I'm going to bake a cake for Mum
   ◯ a) if she is in town.
   ◯ b) while she is in town.

10. Sheila wants to visit her cousin
    ◯ a) before the summer holidays are over.
    ◯ b) as soon as the summer holidays are over.

Übung 2

Choose a verb for each sentence and fill in the correct verb forms.
find – get – get home – come back – arrive

1. As soon as my dad .... from his trip, I'll tell him to give you a ring.
2. I'll be waiting for you at the information desk when you ....
3. We have to clean our rooms before Mum ....
4. John is going to sell his motorbike as soon as he .... a better one.
5. If you answer this question correctly, you .... a good mark.

Übung 3

Brigitte is daydreaming again. Translate into English.

1. Sobald ich genug Geld habe, reise ich um die Welt.

   ....

2. Wenn ich in San Francisco ankomme, besuche ich den Shakespeare Garten im Golden Gate Park.

   ....

   ....

3. Falls mir das Geld ausgeht, arbeite ich als Bedienung im Moscone Center.

   ....

   ....

4. Ehe ich Kalifornien verlasse, fliege ich nach Los Angeles und schaue mir das neue Getty Museum an.

   ....

   ....

5. Wenn ich München verlasse, wird mich meine Mutter bitten: „Vergiss nicht mir jeden Tag eine Mail zu schicken, bevor du ins Bett gehst."

   ....

   ....

6. Bis ich neue Freunde finde, werde ich Heimweh haben.

   ....

7. Ich schicke meinen Freunden viele Briefe, Mails und Ansichtskarten, während ich weg bin.

   ....

   ....

9. Future Perfect und Future Progressive

Das **Future Progressive** (die Verlaufsform in der Zukunft) verwendet man, wenn man ausdrücken will, dass eine Handlung zu einem zukünftigen Zeitpunkt im Verlauf sein wird.

→ *Next week I'll **be swimming** in the sea.*
Nächste Woche schwimme ich schon im Meer.

Das **Future Progressive** steht auch, wenn man besonders höflich und taktvoll sein möchte.

→ *How long **will** you **be staying** in Britain?*
Wie lange haben Sie vor in Großbritannien zu bleiben?

Bildung:
will ('ll) be + ing-Form

Das **Future Perfect** (die vollendete Zukunft) verwendet man, wenn man ausdrücken will, dass etwas zu einem bestimmten Zeitpunkt in der Zukunft geschehen sein wird.

→ *His aunt left him a generous amount of money, but he lives such an extravagant life that he **will** soon **have spent** all her money.*
Seine Tante hinterließ ihm eine großzügige Geldsumme. Aber er führt ein so ausschweifendes Leben, dass er ihr ganzes Geld bald ausgegeben haben wird.

Bildung:
will ('ll) have + Past Participle

Übung 1

What will the boys and girls be doing this time next year? Fill in the correct verb forms.
work – baby-sit – correct – learn – read – repair

1. This time next year Tom .... the sixth volume of "Harry Potter".
2. John .... in his father's shop.
3. This time next year Ted .... the used car he got from his grandfather.
4. My sister Caroline .... as an au pair in the USA.
5. Our teacher .... our English test papers.
6. .... you still .... English?

Übung 2

Tina and Sarah are spending the week after Christmas in a small hotel in the Alps. A lot of things are not as they should be. Complete the English translation.

1. „Bis heute Abend werden Sie die Spinnen aus unserem Badezimmer entfernt haben."

   "Until tonight you .... the spiders from our bathroom."

2. „Sonst werden wir abgereist sein, bevor Sie bis drei zählen können."

   "Otherwise we .... before you can count to three."

3. Tina und Sarah hoffen auch, dass jemand die Heizung repariert haben wird, bis sie zurückkommen.

   Tina and Sarah also hope that somebody .... the central heating until they come back.

4. Bis zum Ende der Woche werden sie einen Beschwerdebrief geschrieben haben.

   By the end of the week they .... a letter of complaint.

Übung 3

The O'Briens have got a pet now: a puppy. Its name is Mr Bean and it keeps the members of the family quite busy. Put the verbs into the future progressive or the future perfect.

Mrs O'Brien: Vivian, I .... (work) tomorrow afternoon. Can you go for a walk with Mr Bean?

Vivian: I think so. I .... (play) squash with Sheila, but we .... (finish) by three o'clock. Then I can take him for a walk. I hope Mr Bean .... (not eat) one of my shoes again when I come home!

Mr O'Brien: By the way, who .... (look) after Mr Bean when we are away for a week in the summer?

Mrs O'Brien: That's all settled. Mrs Croft .... (come) to our house twice a day and she .... (take) Mr Bean for walks regularly.

Mr O'Brien: I hope he .... (learn) not to dig up the flowers in the garden by then. Otherwise Mrs Croft .... (have) the time of her life!

Vivian: I .... (go) to the dogs' school with him twice a week, starting next Thursday. By August he .... (become) a well-behaved dog!

Mr O'Brien: But my hair .... (turn) grey by then! Maybe we shouldn't have named him Mr Bean!

10. Alle Zukunftsformen im Überblick

Zukunftsform	Sprechabsicht	Verwendung
will-Future	Spontane Absichtserklärung	I'**ll open** the window.
going-to-Future	Geplantes Vorhaben	We **are going to have** a party next Saturday.
will-Future	Allgemeine Vorhersage/ Vermutung	You'**ll like** the film.
going-to-Future	Etwas bahnt sich bereits an.	Stop fooling around. You **are going to fall** off that ladder!
Simple Present	Fahrplan, Veranstaltungs-Termin (von anderen festgelegt)	Which platform **does** the train **leave** from? The film **starts** at eight thirty.
Present Progressive	Getroffene Vereinbarung	We **are making** tortillas on Friday evening.
Future Progressive	Andauernde Handlung zu einem Zeitpunkt in der Zukunft Höfliche Anfrage	I'**ll be working** in the afternoon. When **will** you **be moving** to Aberdeen?
Future Perfect	Etwas wird zu einem best. Zeitpunkt geschehen sein.	In two days' time I'**ll have finished** reading the book.

Übung 1

The final exams are drawing nearer at Broughton High School. Um welche Sprechabsicht handelt es sich jeweils? Welche Zukunftsform wird im Englischen verwendet?

	Sprechabsicht	Futurform im Englischen
1. Nächste Woche um diese Zeit werde ich die Prüfung schon geschrieben haben.	....	....
2. Sarah sieht ziemlich müde aus. Sie schläft jede Minute ein.	....	....
3. Morgen zwischen drei und fünf Uhr? Da lerne ich für die Prüfung!	....	....
4. Ich mache mir jetzt eine Tasse Kaffee.	....	....
5. Ich bin sicher wir werden nicht durchfallen.	....	....
6. Nach der Prüfung verbringen Kevin und John eine Woche am Meer.	....	....
7. Wann fängt die Prüfung am Montag an?	....	....
8. Sheila besucht im August ihre Großmutter in Indien.	....	....

Übung 2

Now translate sentences 1–8 into English.

1. ....
2. ....
3. ....
4. ....
5. ....
6. ....
7. ....
8. ....

11. Übungen zu allen Futurformen

Übung 1

Tim and his girlfriend Pat want to go to Berkeley, California, as exchange students for a year. Pat is telling her friend Pamela about her plans. Fill in the correct future forms.

Pat: I've got some good news for you. Tim and I .... (go) to Berkeley as exchange students for a year. And one other thing: Before we .... (leave) we .... (get married) – on August 21st.

Pamela: That's wonderful! I .... (be) your bridesmaid. That is – if you want me.

Pat: Of course I do! You can be sure that I .... (not say) "Yes" if my best friend .... (not be) at my side. The wedding .... (not be) a big one. Nevertheless, there are lots of things that have to be arranged.

Pamela: You can count on me if you .... (need) any help.

Pat: Thanks a lot. My mother .... (write) the invitations. And my brother's band .... (play) at the wedding party. By the way, my 93-year-old great-grandmother .... (come), too.

Pamela: When .... the semester .... (start) at Berkeley?

Pat: It .... (start) exactly one week after our wedding. So we .... (not have) much of a honeymoon!

Pamela: .... you .... (stay) on campus?

Pat: Yes, that .... (make) things a lot easier. By the time all our friends come visiting us we .... (find) places where they can stay without paying a fortune.

Pamela: I .... (miss) you terribly during that year.

Pat: So will I. But I .... (send) you hundreds of postcards and e-mails.

Pamela: When you come back, you .... (get) an American accent.

Pat: Oh, no – we .... But listen: If you .... (not visit) us in Berkeley, I .... (be) really disappointed.
Oh God, it's late. I .... (meet) Tim at four o'clock.

Pamela: Well, then you'd better hurry up! Give him a kiss from me.

Übung 2

What will the year 2060 be like?
Complete the translations by filling in the correct future forms.
Sometimes more than one form is possible.

1. Niemand wird das Haus verlassen müssen, um Essen oder Kleidung zu kaufen.

   Nobody .... the house to buy food or clothes.

2. Alles wird „online" bestellt und sofort geliefert werden.

   Everything .... online and .... immediately.

3. Aussagen wie: „Nächste Woche machen wir einen Ausflug zum Mond." werden nicht ungewöhnlich sein.

   Statements like: "Next week we .... a trip to the moon." .... unusual.

4. „Wie lange haben Sie vor zu bleiben?"

   "How long .... you ....?"

5. „Wir verbringen drei Nächte im Weltraumhotel. Von dort aus machen wir mehrere Tagesausflüge zum Mond."

   "We .... three nights at the space resort. From there we .... several day trips to the moon."

6. „Verzeihung, wann geht die nächste Raumfähre?"

   "Excuse me, when .... the next space shuttle ....?"

7. Auf der Erde wird das Wasser der Flüsse wieder genießbar geworden sein.

   On earth the water in rivers .... drinkable again.

8. Jeder Schüler wird seinen Taschencomputer zum Unterricht mitnehmen. Vielleicht wird das Klassenzimmer ein virtuelles geworden sein.

   Every pupil/student .... his pocket computer to class. Maybe the classroom .... a virtual one.

Englisch 9./10. Klasse

Astrid Stannat, Martina Mattes

If-Sätze und Futurformen

Lösungsteil
(an der Perforation heraustrennen)

Nach dem Heraustrennen bitte hier klammern

Mentor Übungsbuch 856

Mentor Verlag München

A Warming up
1. Die Zeiten: Simple Present, Simple Past, Past Perfect

Übung 1

Air Force One:
In this thriller Harrison Ford plays the US President who finds himself trapped on board a hijacked plane.
The Full Monty:
This smash hit movie is about a group of unemployed Sheffield steel workers who turn to stripping to escape the poverty trap.
McLeod's Daughters:
Set in the Australian outback, this drama traces the fortunes of a daughter who returns to the family farm when her father dies.
One Fine Day:
George Clooney and Michelle Pfeiffer star as two single parents who get through a series of chaotic events.

Übung 2

A million female hearts broke when they came out last year with the news that Dr Doug Ross (George Clooney) would be quitting County General Hospital at the end of the fifth serial. Clooney decided to concentrate on his big screen career.
When the British actress Alex Kingston was offered a role in *Emergency Room*, she didn't find it easy to move to America. While Alex was unsure, *Emergency Room's* producers were not/weren't. "When she walked in, she showed such intelligence and humour that we didn't hesitate one minute." At first Alex didn't like Los Angeles. "But my colleagues really helped me. They are wonderful actors and there's a lot of laughter around the set. They made me feel at home."

Übung 3

She had already bought some ice-cream.
She had already written an essay for school.
She hadn't learned the German words yet.
She hadn't tidied up her room yet.
She had already made a cake.

Hier ein paar nützliche Vokabeln zum Themenbereich *Film und Fernsehen:*

director	Regisseur(in)	character	Figur, Gestalt
viewer	Fernsehzuschauer(in)	plot	Handlung
channel	Programm, Kanal	rating	Einschaltquote
commercial	Werbespot	shot	Aufnahme
feature film	Spielfilm	to shoot a film	einen Film drehen
animated film, cartoon	Zeichentrickfilm	to star somebody	jemanden in einer Hauptrolle zeigen
script	Drehbuch	to go to the pictures (BE)/ movies (AE)	ins Kino gehen
subtitle	Untertitel		
screen	Bildschirm		
programme	Sendung		

2. Regelmäßige und unregelmäßige Verben

8 | 9

Übung 1

Simple Present	Simple Past	Past Perfect
he solves	he solved	he had solved
we don't take	we didn't take	we hadn't taken
they think	they thought	they had thought
you empty	you emptied	you had emptied
she doesn't give	she didn't give	she hadn't given
I don't stop	I didn't stop	I hadn't stopped
he helps	he helped	he had helped
she sees	she saw	she had seen
we move	we moved	we had moved

Übung 2

After they had picked up their luggage, a bus took them to their hotel. They had rooms with a beautiful view of the sea.
After they had spent their first day on the beach, they realized that they all had turned quite red in the hot summer sun. They hadn't used any sunscreen product for their skin – a mistake they didn't make again!
Mrs Northam loves going to museums. On Sunday they visited Malta's capital Valetta. Kevin and Fiona didn't want to spend hours at the National Museum with their parents, so they went to a café instead.
Fiona doesn't like history at school very much, but she was very impressed by the pre-historic temples of Tarxien and Ggantija. She hadn't seen anything like that before.
Kevin and Fiona were very proud of the bargains they had got at the street market in Valetta. Kevin had bought some coins for his collection and Fiona had found a beautiful orange blouse there.

Übung 3

1. Kevin collects all sorts of coins.
2. Mr Northam forgot to leave the key at the hotel reception.
3. Mrs Northam had enjoyed looking at the beautiful sunset.
4. Fiona doesn't understand the language of the Maltese people.

Hier ein paar nützliche Vokabeln zum Thema *Reisen:*

journey, trip	Reise, Fahrt	abroad	im/ins Ausland
package tour	Pauschalreise	to leave for	aufbrechen nach
by car/bus/train	mit dem Auto/Bus/Zug	to pack	(ein)packen
board	Verpflegung	to unpack	auspacken
sights	Sehenswürdigkeiten	to travel	reisen
passport	Reisepass	to hitchhike	per Anhalter fahren
suitcase	Koffer	to book, to reserve	reservieren
return ticket	Rückfahrkarte	to check in	einchecken, ankommen
tourist office	Fremdenverkehrsbüro		
guide	Reiseführer		

3. Zwei Kreuzworträtsel
... und noch mehr unregelmäßige Verben

Übung 1

Simple Past

ACROSS 2. blew, 5. came, 6. brought, 7. thought, 9. began, 10. bet, 13. heard, 14. shut, 15. slept, 16. got, 18. fell, 20. swam, 22. threw, 23. spent, 24. fed, 26. lost, 28. found, 29. sent, 30. met

DOWN 1. understood, 2. bought, 3. broke, 4. caught, 6. became, 8. went, 9. built, 11. wrote, 12. spelt, spelled, 13. had, 14. spoke ,17. beat, 19. left, 20. stood, 21. ate, 23. shone, 25. drove, 27. sang

Übung 2

Past Participles

ACROSS: 2. made, 3. thrown, 7. forgotten, 9. brought, 11. caught, 12. eaten, 14. run, 16. chosen, 17. frozen, 18. stood, 19. kept, 21. bitten, 23. bled, 25. slept, 26. fought, 28. built, 30. torn, 31. given, 32. got, 33. known, 35. begun, 37. driven, 39. found

DOWN: 1. understood, 2. met, 4. won, 5. bought, 6. beaten, 8. fallen, 9. thrown, 10. heard, 13. stolen, 15. spent, 16. cut, 20. dug, 21. broken, 22. been, 24. flown, 25. shown, 27. hidden, 28. blown, 29. hit, 34. worn, 36. drawn, 38. shot

Hier einige wichtige unregelmäßige Verben:

be, was (were), been	sein	give, gave, given	geben
become, became, become	werden	hear, heard, heard	hören
begin, began, begun	beginnen	hold, held, held	halten
bite, bit, bitten	beißen	hurt, hurt, hurt	verletzen, schmerzen
blow, blew, blown	blasen, wehen	know, knew, known	wissen
break, broke, broken	(zer)brechen	learn, learnt, learnt	lernen
bring, brought, brought	(her)bringen	learned, learned	
build, built, built	bauen	leave, left, left	(ver)lassen
buy, bought, bought	kaufen	lend, lent, lent	leihen
catch, caught, caught	fangen	lose, lost, lost	verlieren
choose, chose, chosen	(aus)wählen	mean, meant, meant	bedeuten, meinen
come, came, come	kommen	meet, met, met	(sich) treffen
cost, cost, cost	kosten	pay, paid, paid	bezahlen
cut, cut, cut	schneiden	say, said, said	sagen
do, did, done	tun	see, saw, seen	sehen
dream, dreamt, dreamt	träumen	sell, sold, sold	verkaufen
dreamed, dreamed		show, showed, shown	zeigen
drink, drank, drunk	trinken	smell, smelt, smelt	riechen
drive, drove, driven	fahren	spend, spent, spent	verbringen, ausgeben
eat, ate, eaten	essen	tear, tore, torn	(zer)reißen
feel, felt, felt	(sich) fühlen	think, thought, thought	denken, glauben
find, found, found	finden	throw, threw, thrown	werfen
fly, flew, flown	fliegen	wear, wore, worn	tragen (Kleidung)

B If-Sätze
1. If-Sätze: Grundtypen

Übung 1

1. If my friend in Scotland had a computer, I would send her e-mails instead of ringing her every few days.
2. Kevin would have come to Julia's birthday party in time if his bike hadn't had a puncture.
3. If those cool trousers are still there tomorrow, I'll buy them.
4. Vivian would go to the late show at the cinema if she didn't have a test tomorrow.
5. If Jomo hadn't sprained his ankle, he would have taken part in the skateboard competition last weekend.

Übung 2

1. If my friend in Scotland had a computer … type II
2. Kevin would have come to Julia's birthday party in time … type III
3. If those cool trousers are still there tomorrow … type I
4. Vivian would go to the late show at the cinema … type II
5. If Jomo hadn't sprained his ankle … type III

Übung 3

1. If I work at the sports shop, I will get a new pair of trainers at a cheaper price.
2. Alicia will get good tips if the manager of the golf club employs her as a waitress.
3. If Pete had a motorbike, he would apply for a job at Safeway's supermarket. It's definitely too far to go by bike.
4. I would work at the take-away if they paid a little more.
5. If Kevin hadn't broken his leg last summer, he would have worked at the car wash.
6. I certainly wouldn't have minded the Sullivans' kids if I had known that they never went to bed before eleven o'clock!

Hier ein paar nützliche Vokabeln zum Thema *Arbeit und Beruf:*

apprentice	Auszubildende(r)	full-time	Vollzeit-, Ganztags-
employer	Arbeitgeber(in)	part-time	Teilzeit-
employee	Arbeitnehmer(in)	out of work, unemployed	arbeitslos
boss	Chef(in), Arbeitgeber(in)		
working hours	Arbeitszeit	temporary	vorübergehend
pay	Bezahlung	to have a day off	einen Tag frei haben
department	Abteilung	to apply	sich bewerben
office	Büro, Amt	to earn one's living	seinen Lebensunterhalt verdienen
job interview	Vorstellungsgespräch		
flexitime	gleitende Arbeitszeit	to afford	sich leisten (können)

14 15

2. *If you need any help …*
If-Sätze – Typ I

Übung 1

1. If you are interested in theatre and acting, you can/might join the drama group.
2. If you are ill, you or your parents must inform the school.
3. If you like music and dancing, you can/might come to one of our school discos.
4. If your parents take you to school by car, they shouldn't drive into the school grounds because there isn't much parking space there.
5. If you are keen on earrings, don't wear more than one in one ear! Nose or eye brow studs aren't allowed, either!
6. If you and your parents want to know more about the school, you will/can/might find lots of interesting pieces of information in the "Broughton Bulletin" – that's our quarterly newsletter.

Übung 2

1. If we don't find any sponsors, we won't have any prizes for the song contest.
2. We could hold a skateboard competition if it doesn't rain.
3. If there aren't any refreshments, the visitors won't stay long.
4. My uncle will lend us his stereo equipment if we don't let anybody else get near it.
5. If we offer a number of different activities, people won't have to queue up all the time.

Übung 3

1. My sister will lend you her bike if we want to go on a bike trip.
2. If you don't like bike trips, we can go swimming.
3. One other thing: We'll go to an open air concert if my friend gets tickets.
4. If you've got enough space in your suitcase, bring your roller skates!
5. If Dad doesn't have time / If Dad hasn't got time, Mum will go to a theme park with us.

Hier ein paar nützliche Vokabeln zum Thema *Aussehen:*

beauty	Schönheit	pretty	hübsch
appearance	Aussehen	fair	blond
figure	Figur	dark	dunkel(haarig)
haircut	Haarschnitt	slender, slim	schlank
suntan	Sonnenbräune	fat	dick, fettleibig
necklace	Halsband	pale	blass
earring	Ohrring	smart	schick, elegant
stud	(Ohr-)Stecker, Piercing	neat	ordentlich, gepflegt
handsome	gutaussehend	to put on	anziehen
beautiful	schön, hübsch	to get ready	(sich) fertig machen
attractive	attraktiv	to try on	anprobieren

16 | 17

3. *If a fairy granted me one wish …*
If-Sätze – Typ II

Übung 1

1. John wouldn't be so successful if he didn't train three or four times a week.
2. If John and Vivian had tickets for Wimbledon, they might/could/would watch André Agassi live for the first time.
3. If the firm John's father works for didn't sponsor his son, John's sport would be too expensive for the Websters.
4. John would finish school even if he earned a lot of money as a professional tennis player.
5. His girlfriend Vivian would love him even if he didn't win every match.

Übung 2

Vivian: If you went out with your brother and his boyfriend, and if your brother pretended to be tired and went home, "he" might give you a lift.
Sheila: If I were you, I'd/would wear that terrific blue top!
Jennifer: If I didn't have those braces, I'd/would be more self-confident.
Vivian: Honestly – if I had your looks, I wouldn't worry about braces!

Übung 3

Chris (16): If I had a motorbike, it wouldn't take hours to get to school.
Judy (14): If we didn't have school in the afternoon, I could / would meet my friends more often.
Sarah (15): If I became a Hollywood star, I would have dinner with Leonardo di Caprio.
Richard (15): If I won a free trip to the moon, I would send my geography teacher a postcard.

Hier ein paar nützliche Vokabeln zum Wortfeld *Gefühle und Beziehungen:*

feelings	Gefühle	to get to know	kennen lernen
a good sense of humour	Sinn für Humor	to be fond of	gern, lieb haben
trust	Vertrauen	to be in a good/bad mood	gute/schlechte Laune haben
happy	glücklich	to miss	vermissen
sad	traurig	to quarrel	streiten
glad	froh	to lie	lügen
upset	durcheinander, aufgeregt	to chat	plaudern
excited	aufgeregt	to apologize	sich entschuldigen
angry (about)	ärgerlich, verärgert (über)	to trust	vertrauen
mad (about)	wütend (über)	I can't stand …	ich kann … nicht ertragen
jealous	eifersüchtig		
disappointed	enttäuscht	to fancy	mögen

18 19

4. *If or when?* Bedingung oder Zeitpunkt?

Übung 1

1. Nebensatz der Zeit
2. Bedingungssatz
3. Nebensatz der Zeit
4. Nebensatz der Zeit
5. Bedingungssatz
6. Nebensatz der Zeit

Übung 2

1. When Sheila got an invitation from her aunt in Boston, she was very excited.
2. She wrote: "If you don't miss your parents and your friends, I would suggest that you stay for four weeks."
3. "When you arrive, I will pick you up at the airport."
4. "Of course you can call your parents immediately when we get to my place.
5. If Sheila's aunt didn't have internet access, Sheila's boyfriend couldn't send her any e-mails.
6. When Sheila is at the airport, she will have enough time for drinking a cup of coffee before the departure.

Übung 3

1. Chris calls Sheila almost every day when she comes/gets home from school.
2. When she told him about her trip to America, he was not very enthusiastic.
3. Chris asked: "If you got to know a nice boy in Boston, would you fall in love with him?".
4. Sheila's answer: "If you don't stop asking such silly/stupid questions, I'll send you a photo of me and Leonardo di Caprio!".
5. Chris laughed. "O.K.! When I come back from basketball practice, I'll pick you up and we'll go to the cinema – 'The Beach' with Leonardo di Caprio is on at the moment!".

Hier ein paar nützliche Vokabeln zum Wortfeld *Flughafen:*

arrival	Ankunft	to take off	starten, abheben
departure	Abflug	to land	landen
hand luggage (BE)	Handgepäck	plane, aircraft	Flugzeug
hand baggage (AE)		wing	Tragfläche
baggage claim	Gepäckausgabe	flight attendant	Flugbegleiter(in)
customs	Zoll	runway	Start-/Landebahn
passport control	Passkontrolle	delayed	verspätet
announcement	Durchsage	cancelled	abgesagt, storniert

20 21

5. *Mixed exercises:* If-Sätze – Typ I und Typ II

Übung 1

1. If I were you, I'd join a cycling club. That's great fun and you can learn a lot!
2. If you want to buy a second-hand bike, check the main mountain bike magazines for classified ads.
3. If you haven't got a helmet, you should look for a good one that fits perfectly.
4. If I didn't have to study for that maths test, I'd go to the bike shop with you.
5. If you intend to ride regularly, cycling shorts are a must. They have a padded insert and make cycling much more comfortable.

Übung 2

Sheila:	If you allow me to go out tonight, I'll/I will be back at midnight, I promise.
Mrs Ragunathan:	If you didn't go out so often, you could have much better marks at school.
Sheila:	But Mum! If I only stayed at home, life would be terribly boring and I wouldn't study more than I do now! I promise – if you let me go out tonight, I won't go out tomorrow.
Mrs Ragunathan:	If you showed just a little more enthusiasm for your school subjects, I wouldn't have anything to worry about.
Sheila:	If Sheila Ragunathan doesn't get an A or a B in her next test, she won't go out for a whole month. Is that a deal?
Mrs Ragunathan:	That sounds fine.

Übung 3

1. John: If somebody has got today's newspaper, we can/could/might have a look what's on at the cinema.
2. Alison: If the new James Bond film is on, don't count me in! I hate James Bond!
3. Chris: If we lived in London, we would be able to go to the fairground at the Millennium Dome.
4. Sheila: The Escape Club would be a nice place to go to if they didn't play such terrible music!
5. Alison: If you are hungry, we can have a snack first. There's a new Italian pasta bar in Lancaster Road.
6. Sheila: I can only go there if somebody lends me five pounds.
7. John: O.K. – if we all hurry up, we 'll catch/will catch the bus!

Hier ein paar nützliche Vokabeln zum Themenbereich *Erholung, Spiel, Sport:*

recreation	Erholung	to score	(Punkte) erzielen
leisure, spare time	Freizeit		(Tore) schießen
pleasure	Vergnügen	to take part in	teilnehmen an
athlete	Sportler(in), Athlet(in)	to hit	schlagen, treffen
event	Ereignis, Veranstaltung	to run	laufen
gymnasium	Turnhalle	to jump	springen, hüpfen
rule	Regel	to have fun	Spaß haben
tournament	Turnier	indoors	drinnen
spectator	Zuschauer(in)	outdoor games	Spiele im Freien

22 | 23

6. *If things had been different …*
If-Sätze – Typ III

Übung 1

1. If Anakin Skywalker had been a girl in "Star Wars: Episode I", she would have been the first female Jedi knight.
2. Fewer hankies would have become soaked with tears if Leonardo di Caprio had survived in "Titanic".
3. If Shakespeare hadn't fallen in love, his career as a playwright would/might/could have come to a quick end.
4. Mr Bean's American host family wouldn't have protested if he had moved out of their house.
5. If Arnold Schwarzenegger hadn't shown his muscles in his latest film, it might have become a flop.
6. Julia Roberts wouldn't have fallen in love with Hugh Grant in *Notting Hill* if he hadn't spilled his orange juice on her T-shirt.
7. If Rhett Butler hadn't looked so handsome, Scarlett O'Hara mightn't have fallen for him.

Übung 2

If I hadn't missed the bus, I wouldn't have got my motorbike out of the garden-shed. If I hadn't got my motorbike out of the garden-shed, I wouldn't have torn my new jacket. If I hadn't torn my new jacket, I wouldn't have been so furious and I wouldn't have kicked my motorbike. If I hadn't kicked my motorbike, it wouldn't have fallen on my foot. If my motorbike hadn't fallen on my foot, I wouldn't have played badly at the football match. If I hadn't played badly at the football match, my team wouldn't have lost the match."

Übung 3

If John had studied harder, he wouldn't have made so many mistakes.
If he had not been partying all night, he would have kept a clear head.
If he hadn't forgotten his watch, time wouldn't have run out for him.
John's father would have studied with him if he had asked him.

Hier ein paar nützliche Vokabeln zum Wortfeld *Schule:*

education	Erziehung, Bildung	blackboard	Wandtafel
elementary school	Grundschule	subject	Unterrichtsfach
public school (BE)	Privatschule mit Internat	break	Pause
comprehensive school	Gesamtschule	staff room	Lehrerzimmer
boarding school	Internat	to attend	besuchen (Schule)
high school, grammar school	weiterführende Schule	to cheat	mogeln
		to pass	schaffen, bestehen
exam	Prüfung	to fail	nicht bestehen, durchfallen
report	Zeugnis		
mark (BE), grade (AE)	Note	to mark	zensieren, bewerten

7. *Mixed exercises* – Typ I, II und III

24 25

Übung 1

1. Even if John and his father didn't catch any fish, they would have a lot of fun together.
2. They will go on a fishing holiday next summer if it doesn't cost a fortune.
3. They would have gone last spring if John hadn't caught a bad cold.
4. If John didn't have to be out at the crack of dawn, he would enjoy their fishing trips even more.
5. If they had a boat, they could go out onto the river and fish in different areas.
6. John's father wouldn't have become soaking wet last weekend if he hadn't slipped and fallen into the water.

Übung 2

Type I: John's father can't go fishing with his son in the holidays if he doesn't get a day off from work.
Type II: John's father couldn't go fishing with his son in the holidays if he didn't get a day off from work.
Type III: John's father couldn't have gone fishing with his son in the holidays if he hadn't got a day off from work.

Type I: If Fiona finds a well-paid summer job, she will buy a new stereo.
Type II: If Fiona found a well-paid summer job, she would buy a new stereo.
Type III: If Fiona had found a well-paid summer job, she would have bought a new stereo.

Type I: John will bring us some pizzas if the take-away round the corner is open.
Type II: John would bring us some pizzas if the take-away round the corner was open.
Type III: John would have brought us some pizzas if the take-away round the corner had been open.

Type I: If it doesn't rain, the Hendersons will go camping.
Type II: If it didn't rain, the Hendersons would go camping.
Type III: If it hadn't rained, the Hendersons would have gone camping.

Übung 3

On the top of a high mountain in the Austrian Alps there is a sign warning climbers: "Be careful not to fall. It's a dangerous place. But if you fall, look to the right. The Alps are beautiful!"
A young lady is standing in front of her wardrobe complaining to her husband: "Just look at my clothes. If anyone came they might think I was a cook. Her husband replies calmly: "If they stayed for dinner they wouldn't!"

26 27 8. *More mixed exercises* – Typ I, II und III

Übung 1

If Britney Spears hadn't been such a talented young girl, she wouldn't have become a TV star at 11. Her music videos wouldn't have earned so much praise if she hadn't taken dance classes for years. If her single and album sales continue to break records, she will become a big star.
Robbie Williams would be an actor now if he hadn't responded to the newspaper ad of a band some years ago. If Robbie hadn't drunk too much, he wouldn't have dived into the fountain of a hotel and he wouldn't have a scar just above his eyes now.

Übung 2

If Jeremy hadn't joined the local cycling club two years ago, he wouldn't be so good at this sport now. If he trains hard, he can win the cross-country course next month. And if Jeremy wins the competition, a local helmet manufacturer will sponsor him for two years.
Jeremy and his friends usually ride in the Forest Enterprise woodlands where there are marked trails for cyclists. If they didn't have good cycling equipment, their parents wouldn't let them do this sport. Last year Jeremy fell off his bike and would have hurt himself badly if he hadn't had such a good helmet.
When Jeremy visits his cousin Greg next weekend, Greg will show him the most exciting trails in the area.

Übung 3

Sharon: I heard that you can be an au pair if you are between 18 and 30 years old – is that right?
Vivian: Yes, that's true. And you don't have to be a girl! If I had enough money, I would go to the United States for a holiday. But if I work as an au pair, I will get pocket money and I won't have to pay anything for room and board.
Sharon: Can you switch families if you don't get along with your host family?
Vivian: Yes, you can. Your au pair agency will help you. That's why it's important to find an agency that belongs to an international au pair organization.
By the way – if I didn't have any childcare experience, I wouldn't be accepted by some agencies.
Sharon: If my sister's friend had gathered more information about being an au pair, I'm sure she wouldn't have had such a negative experience.
Vivian: If I like the States, maybe I 'll stay there!
Sharon: If I didn't have such a fear of flying, I would come with you.

Übung 4

1. If you don't like children and housework, you shouldn't work as an au pair.
2. Many au pairs would not be so surprised if they had chosen their host family more carefully.
3. If I had been under 21, it would have been much more difficult for me in the USA to go out in the evening.

9. *If only ...* – Irreale Wunschsätze

28 29

Übung 1

1. I wish I didn't have a temperature.
2. If only my throat didn't hurt so much.
3. I wish Sheila were/was here.
4. Wasn't that the doorbell? If only someone came to visit me.
5. I wish I felt better. I can't even read a book.
6. If only the hours passed a little more quickly.
7. If only those church bells didn't ring every quarter of an hour.

Übung 2

1. If only I had made more sandwiches.
2. I wish Pete hadn't talked so much.
3. If only Jomo hadn't dropped a full bottle of coke.
4. I wish Susan had played a few songs on the guitar.
5. If only I had asked Karen to bring some of her CDs.
6. I wish Steve had complimented me on my new dress.

Übung 3

Alison: If only the rain stopped.
Roger: I wish we had packed our raincoats.
Kevin: If only we had watched the weather forecast.
Sheila: I wish I didn't have wet feet.
Jomo: If only I found my cards. Then we could play a game of rummy.
John: I wish you didn't complain about everything.

Hier ein paar nützliche Vokabeln zum Wortfeld *Gesundheit und Krankheit:*

health	Gesundheit	painful	schmerzhaft
illness, disease	Krankheit	contagious	ansteckend
injury	Verletzung	severe	schlimm, stark
pain	Schmerz	to suffer from	leiden an
bandage	Verband	to recover	sich erholen, gesund werden
prescription	Rezept		
medical treatment	medizin. Versorgung	I feel sick.	Mir ist übel.
recovery	Genesung	to bleed	bluten
breakdown	Zusammenbruch	to faint	ohnmächtig werden
flu	Grippe	to catch (a) cold	sich erkälten
headache	Kopfschmerzen	to hurt	schmerzen, weh tun

30 | 31

10. *Had it stopped raining …*
Verdrehte Bedingungssätze

Übung 1

1. If you should want to watch a bilingual programme, you can select the language.
2. If the remote control unit shouldn't operate, change the batteries.
3. If there should be any recording trouble, the clock time might not be set correctly.
4. If the sound quality should be poor, the tape might be defective.

Übung 2

Mr Webster: Had the boy's father not gone for a walk with his son in such stormy weather, this wouldn't have happened.
Mrs Webster: Had they not walked so close to the edge of the cliff, it wouldn't have been so dangerous.
John: Had the boy fallen into the water, he might have drowned.
Mrs Webster: Had it taken longer to call for help, the boy might have died.
Sarah: Had the RAF helicopter crew not been so excellent, they might not have been able to rescue the boy from the bottom of the cliffs.

Übung 3

1. Had he practised with his new skateboard a little longer, this wouldn't have happened.
2. Had he not jumped into the air, he wouldn't have fallen.
3. Should he try to skate with his broken arm, his mother would hide his skateboard.

Hier ein paar nützliche Vokabeln zum Wortfeld *Wetter und Klima:*

weather	Wetter	fine, beautiful, fair	schön
storm	Sturm	bad, nasty	schlecht, garstig
thunderstorm	Gewitter	cool	kühl
lightning	Blitz	chilly	frostig
blizzard	Schneesturm	hot	heiß
hurricane	Orkan	foggy	neblig
cold	Kälte	cloudy	bewölkt
warmth	Wärme	it is clearing up	es hellt sich auf
sunny spells	sonnige Abschnitte	to rain	regnen
(weather) forecast	Wetterbericht	to pour	schütten

C Futurformen
1. Spontane Absichtserklärung: will-Future

32 | 33

Übung 1

1. John: I'll go to the information desk over there.
2. Jomo: I'll have a look at the timetable.
3. John: I think I'll buy one of those T-shirts.
   Jomo: I don't think I'll get one.
4. John: I'll be right back.

Übung 2

1. I'll return the books for you.
2. I think I'll go to the dentist's.
3. I don't think I'll invite 20 guests to my party. / I won't invite 20 guests to my party.
4. I'll ring Robert and ask him if he wants to come along.
5. I don't think I'll ride again. / I won't ride again.

Übung 3

1. John: The first thing that I'll do – I'll take a shower.
2. Kevin: I'll put up our certificate in the classroom.
3. Samantha: I think I'll eat three portions of spaghetti.
4. Sheila: I don't think I'll touch a ball again today. / I don't think I'll touch another ball today.
5. Jomo: I'll go home and watch the Star Wars video.
6. Vivian: I'll put ice on my thumb. It's pretty swollen.

Hier ein paar nützliche Vokabeln zum Thema *Fußball:*

team	Mannschaft, Team	forward	Stürmer
captain	Mannschaftskapitän	defender	Verteidiger
coach	Trainer	goalkeeper (goalie)	Torwart
championship	Meisterschaft		
Cup Final	Pokalendspiel	penalty kick	Elfmeter
fan, supporter	Fan, Anhänger	to score a goal	ein Tor schießen
hooligan	Fußballrowdy	scoreboard	Anzeigetafel
referee	Schiedsrichter	goal line	Torlinie
linesman	Linienrichter	result	Ergebnis, Resultat

34 | 35

2. Geplantes Vorhaben: going-to-Future

Übung 1

10	12	14	16
The Taylors	The Hendersons	The O'Sullivans	The Campbells
are going to have a barbecue party.	are going to paint their kitchen.	are going to visit friends in York.	are going to buy a new computer.

Übung 2

1. Alison is going to work at Safeway's supermarket.
2. Greg and Laura are going to go to an open-air concert.
3. Steve is going to take part in a kite festival in Coventry.
4. Gloria is going to attend a language course in France.
5. Patrick is going to spend two weeks in a summer camp in Wales.

Übung 3

1. I'm not going to start studying the last day before the exam.
2. I'm going to learn words for a quarter of an hour every day.
3. I'm going to buy a book with exercises and I'm going to do a few exercises every weekend.
4. On Saturday I'm not going to sleep till 11 o'clock, but I'm going to get up at 8.
5. I'm going to give my German teacher an essay to correct every week.

Hier ein paar nützliche Vokabeln zum Wortfeld *Familie:*

family	Familie	relative	Verwandter
child (pl. children)	Kind	parent	Elternteil (Vater o. Mutter)
wife (pl. wives)	Ehefrau	single parent	allein erziehender Elternteil
husband	Ehemann	grandmother	Großmutter
mother	Mutter	grandchild	Enkel
daughter	Tochter	marital status	Familienstand
son	Sohn	single	ledig
grandparents	Großeltern	married	verheiratet
grandfather	Großvater	divorced	geschieden
aunt	Tante	to get engaged	sich verloben
uncle	Onkel	to get married	heiraten
niece	Nichte	to bring up/ to raise	erziehen, aufziehen
nephew	Neffe		

3. Allgemeine Vorhersage oder Vermutung: will-Future

36 37

Übung 1

1. Tomorrow there will be some heavy rain showers in the north of Scotland. The temperature will fall below 8°C and you will need warm clothes.
2. Strong winds will come from the east. They will blow away the clouds in the late afternoon.
3. The sun won't find any clouds to hide behind on Saturday. The winds will calm down and the temperature will rise to 18°C.
4. Sunday will bring excellent weather for all kinds of outdoor activities. It will be sunny and warm all day with temperatures rising to 22°C.

Übung 2

1. I'm sure you will be impressed by the castle.
2. You will probably taste a whisky at the Scotch Whisky Heritage Centre.
3. I expect you will spend some time at the waterfront.
4. I'm sure you will try out lots of excellent restaurants, bistros and pubs.
5. I expect you will visit The Tavern, the oldest pub in Scotland.
6. I hope you will have lots of fun.

Übung 3

1. Next week you will be surprised by a dear friend.
2. The next weekend/Next weekend will be very exciting for you.
3. You will get a letter which will change your life.
4. Between the 14th and the 18th you will meet an old friend.
5. Your dream partner will step into your life, but you won't see him at first.
6. In the summer one of your dreams will come true.
7. Your purse/wallet won't stay empty for long.

Hier ein paar nützliche Begriffe zum Thema *Horoskop:*

sign of the Zodiac star sign	Sternzeichen	libra	Waage
celestial bodies	Himmelskörper	scorpio	Skorpion
taurus	Stier	sagittarius	Schütze
gemini	Zwillinge	capricorn	Steinbock
cancer	Krebs	aquarius	Wassermann
leo	Löwe	pisces	Fische
virgo	Jungfrau	aries	Widder

38 39 4. Es bahnt sich etwas an: going-to-Future

Übung 1

1. Vivian feels terrible. She thinks she's going to be sick.
2. Look at James Bond's sports car! It's going to explode in a second.
3. Take an umbrella with you. It's going to rain soon.
4. Today there is more traffic in the streets than usual. I think I'm going to be late for work.
5. Those football players look very tired. The other team is going to score a goal any minute.
6. There was an accident in Preston Road. The ambulance is going to arrive soon.
7. Don't park your car here. You are going to get a ticket.
8. John is running round the corner. He's going to catch the bus.

Übung 2

Claire: This is going to be a really trendy area.
Peter: You are going to fall into the water!
Claire: And you are going to rescue me, aren't you?
Peter: I'm hungry – and I 'm not going to look at another seafood restaurant without going in.

Übung 3

Claire: You are going to feel cold pretty soon.
Peter: I'm going to sit very close to you.
Claire: They are going to have fantastic prices in the shops.
Peter: It is going to look terrific on you!

Übung 4

1. A helicopter is going to come and rescue him.
2. We are going to hear a terrible scream.
3. The car is going to overturn.
4. They are going to fall in love with each other.

Hier ein paar nützliche Vokabeln zum Thema *Umweltschutz:*

ecology	Umweltforschung	environment	Umwelt
pollution	Verschmutzung	poison	Gift, Schadstoff
noise	Lärm	harm	Schaden
recycling	Wiederverwertung	survival	Überleben
litter, rubbish, garbage, waste	Abfall, Müll	to protect	(be)schützen
		to pollute	verschmutzen

5. Will-Future oder going-to-Future?

Übung 1

Samantha: I'm going to visit my German pen-friend in August. Maybe I'll find a nice present for her.
Sheila: You will speak German fluently when you come back. Look, they sell power bead bracelets over there. I'll get a pink one for myself – that's for love and romance.
Samantha: That's a nice cardigan. I'll try it on.
Sheila: Give me your bag. I'll hold it for you. Be careful – that pile of T-shirts is going to fall.
Samantha: What are you going to wear at Jill's birthday next week?
Sheila: I don't know yet. I hope I'll find something nice here on the market.

Übung 2

1. I'm going to do a course in computer programming.
2. Do you think I'll be able to make my own Internet homepage soon?
3. Why don't we start our own Internet business? I'm sure we'll make a lot of money.
4. My dad is going to contact a business partner in California.
5. I'm pretty sure he'll offer me a holiday job.
6. There will be a growing demand for web designers in the future.

Übung 3

Jeff: Kevin and I have already decided what we are going to do. Kevin is going to send an e-mail to the World Land Trust and ask for material. I'm going to collect articles about the rainforest in Brazil.
Jennifer: I'm sure people will want to get information about environmental projects in Britain, too.
Eve: That's a good idea. My uncle is a ranger. I'll phone him and interview him about his job. I expect he'll know about projects in the area.
Oliver: I've collected some walkabout leaflets for discovering the local countryside. I'm going to cut out the pictures and maps and make a poster.
Jennifer: By the way – Ms Leigh is going to let us use some geography lessons for preparing the project.

42 | 43

6. Das Simple Present bei Fahrplänen und Öffnungszeiten

Übung 1

1. The plane leaves/takes off at 6 o'clock in the morning.
2. We don't have to change/We needn't change, it's a direct flight.
3. The flight takes 13 hours.
4. We arrive at the hotel at about 10 o'clock local time.
5. The first day of our stay is a bank holiday in the USA.
6. It's a pity that the theatre festival doesn't start a week earlier.

Übung 2

1. When does the Tate Gallery open tomorrow morning?
2. Do the sightseeing buses go every hour this afternoon?
3. Does the 11.15 train to Windsor leave from Victoria station?
4. When does the train arrive at Windsor?
5. What time does the football match Arsenal vs. Leeds start?
6. When do the big department stores close tonight?

Übung 3

Susanne: Harry, when do your summer holidays end?
Harry: On September the first school starts again – and I'm already looking forward to it.
Susanne: How do you get back to Hogwarts Castle? By magic power?
Harry: No, by train. The Hogwarts Express leaves at 11 o'clock from platform nine and three-quarters and arrives at Hogwarts Castle in the evening.
Susanne: Are you allowed to stay up longer on the first evening?
Harry: No, the light is switched/turned off at 11 p.m.

Hier ein paar nützliche Vokabeln zum Thema *Wohnen:*

home	Wohnung, Zuhause	flat	(Etagen-)Wohnung
rent	Miete	to rent	mieten, pachten
landlord	Vermieter	gate	Tor
landlady	Vermieterin	ceiling	Zimmerdecke
floor	Fußboden	hall	Diele, Flur
cellar	Keller	basement	Untergeschoss
view	Aussicht	heating	Heizung
furniture	Möbel	carpet	Teppich
furnished	möbliert	terraced house	Reihenhaus
downstairs	unten, hinunter	semi-detached house	Doppelhaus
upstairs	oben, hinauf		

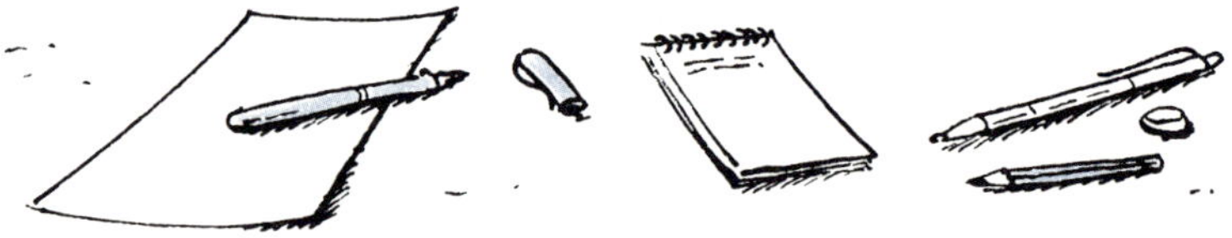

44 45

7. Feste Vereinbarung: Present Progressive

Übung 1

1. Jomo is playing golf with Gerald and Steve on Sunday afternoon.
2. He is meeting Vivian in town on Monday afternoon.
3. He is watching a football match on Tuesday evening.
4. He is going to the dentist's on Wednesday afternoon.
5. He is having a driving lesson on Thursday afternoon.
6. He is helping John repair his motorbike on Friday evening.

Übung 2

1. Mum, Dad and I are flying to Majorca in August.
2. My brother Jim isn't coming with us.
3. He's going camping in Wales with some friends.
4. Some friends of ours are joining us in the second week.
5. What are you doing in the summer holidays?

Übung 3

1.	Mrs O'Brien:	Vivian, the Tylers are having a barbecue party next Saturday. Would you like to come along?
	Vivian:	Yes, I'd love to. What time does it start?
2.	Geena:	Hi, Steve. Jack and I are playing crazy golf this afternoon. Are you coming with us?
	Steve:	Sorry, I'm helping Brian paint his room.
3.	Samantha:	Dad, we are going on an excursion on Tuesday. Could you give me and Sheila a lift to the station? The train leaves at 7.30 a.m.
	Mr Henderson:	OK. Tell Sheila that we are picking her up at 7.
4.	Kevin:	What time does school start tomorrow?
	Jomo:	It starts at 9.45.
5.	Announcement:	Due to reconstruction work in progress the 9.30 train to Manchester does not leave from platform 3 today, but from platform 8.

Hier ein paar nützliche Vokabeln zum Thema *Denken, Verstand:*

mind	Geist, Verstand	conscience	Gewissen
reason	Verstand, Vernunft	truth	Wahrheit
meaning	Bedeutung	sense	Sinn
nonsense	Unsinn	joke	Witz
wisdom	Weisheit	experience	Erfahrung
knowledge	Wissen	basic knowledge	Grundwissen
misunderstanding	Missverständnis	confusion	Verwirrung
dull	dumm, langweilig	stupid	dumm, blöd
bright	intelligent	clever	begabt, gescheit
wise	weise	crazy	verrückt
mad	irre, verrückt	silly	albern
sensible, reasonable	vernünftig	to realize	wahrnehmen

46 47

8. Nebensätze mit *if, when, as soon as, before, until* und *while*

Übung 1

1. b) I'll come to see you before you leave.
2. a) I can't wait till he comes.
3. b) Mr Jackson will complain about his neighbour's dog if it doesn't stop barking.
4. a) Mrs Burnes will be very angry when she sees that her children have smashed her favourite flower pot.
5. a) As soon as we go to bed there will be this strange noise coming from the attic.
6. b) We'll have to stay up until the last guest leaves the house.
7. a) I 'll let you know as soon as I hear from my boyfriend.
8. b) Don't say anything before you know the whole story.
9. b) I'm going to bake a cake for Mum while she is in town.
10. a) Sheila wants to visit her cousin before the summer holidays are over.

Übung 2

1. As soon as my dad comes back from his trip, I'll tell him to give you a ring.
2. I'll be waiting for you at the information desk when you arrive.
3. We have to clean our rooms before Mum gets home.
4. John is going to sell his motorbike as soon as he finds a better one.
5. If you answer this question correctly, you will get a good mark.

Übung 3

1. As soon as I have enough money I'll travel around the world.
2. When I arrive in San Francisco, I'll (I'm going to) visit the Shakespeare Garden at Golden Gate Park.
3. If I run out of money, I'll work as a waitress at the Moscone Center.
4. Before I leave California, I'll (I'm going to) fly to Los Angeles and visit the new Getty Museum.
5. When I leave Munich, my mother will ask me: "Don't forget to send me a mail every day before you go to bed.
6. I'll be homesick until I find new friends.
7. I'm going to send a lot of letters, mails and postcards to my friends while I'm away.

Hier ein paar nützliche Vokabeln zum Wortfeld *Länder, Sprache:*

country	Land	continent	Erdteil
nationality	Nationalität	language	Sprache
Europe	Europa	Asia	Asien
Australia	Australien	Africa	Afrika
North America	Nordamerika	Central America	Mittelamerika
South America	Südamerika	New Zealand	Neuseeland

9. Future Perfect und Future Progressive

48 | 49

Übung 1

1. This time next year Tom will be reading the sixth volume of *"Harry Potter"*.
2. John will be working in his father's shop.
3. This time next year Ted will be repairing the used car he got from his grandfather.
4. My sister Caroline will be babysitting as an au pair in the USA.
5. Our teacher will be correcting our English test-papers.
6. Will you still be learning English?

Übung 2

1. Tonight you will have removed the spiders from our bathroom.
2. Otherwise we will have left before you can count to three.
3. Tina and Sarah also hope that somebody will have repaired the central heating when they come back.
4. By the end of the week they will have written a letter of complaint.

Übung 3

Mrs O'Brien: Vivian, I'll be working tomorrow afternoon. Can you go for a walk with Mr Bean?

Vivian: I think so. I'll be playing squash with Sheila, but we 'll have finished by three o'clock. Then I can take him for a walk. I hope Mr Bean will not/ won't have eaten one of my shoes again when I come home!

Mr O'Brien: By the way, who will be looking after Mr Bean when we are away for a week in the summer?

Mrs O'Brien: That's all settled. Mrs Croft will be coming to our house twice a day and she'll be taking Mr Bean for walks regularly.

Mr O'Brien: I hope he will have learned/learnt not to dig up the flowers in the garden by then. Otherwise Mrs Croft will be having the time of her life!

Vivian: I'll be going to the dogs' school with him twice a week, starting next Thursday. By August he will have become a well-behaved dog!

Mr O'Brien: But my hair will have turned grey by then! Maybe we shouldn't have named him Mr Bean!

Hier ein paar nützliche *Phrasal Verbs:*

get along	vorankommen, auskommen	put off	verschieben
get off	aussteigen aus (Bus, Zug)	put on	anziehen, einschalten
get on	einsteigen	put out	löschen, abschalten
get together	sich treffen	put through	(am Telefon) jemanden verbinden
get up	aufstehen	put up	aufstellen, aufhängen
look after	aufpassen auf	put up with	sich abfinden mit
look ahead	nach vorne blicken	run across s. o.	jemanden zufällig treffen
look for	suchen	run against	sich stoßen an, (politisch:) kandidieren gegen
look up	hinaufblicken, nachschlagen (im Wörterbuch)	run off with	durchbrennen mit
		I've run out of money	Mir ist das Geld ausgegangen.

50 | 51 10. Alle Zukunftsformen im Überblick

Übung 1

	Sprechabsicht	Futurform im Englischen
1. Nächste Woche um diese Zeit werde ich die Prüfung schon geschrieben haben.	Etwas wird zu einem best. Zeitpunkt geschehen sein.	Future Perfect
2. Sarah sieht ziemlich müde aus. Sie schläft jede Minute ein.	Etwas bahnt sich bereits an.	going-to-Future
3. Morgen zwischen drei und fünf Uhr? Da lerne ich für die Prüfung!	Andauernde Handlung in der Zukunft	Future Progressive
4. Ich mache mir jetzt eine Tasse Kaffee.	Spontane Absichtserklärung	will-Future
5. Ich bin sicher wir werden nicht durchfallen.	Allg. Vorhersage	will-Future
6. Nach der Prüfung verbringen Kevin und John eine Woche am Meer.	Geplantes Vorhaben Getroffene Vereinbarung	going-to-Future Present Progressive
7. Wann fängt die Prüfung am Montag an?	Von anderen festgelegter Termin	Simple Present
8. Sheila besucht im August ihre Großmutter in Indien.	Geplantes Vorhaben Getroffene Vereinbarung	going-to-Future Present Progressive

Übung 2

1. This time next week I will already have written the exam.
2. Sarah looks pretty tired. She's going to fall asleep any minute.
3. Tomorrow between three and five o'clock? I'll be studying for the exam!
4. I'll make myself a cup of coffee now.
5. I'm sure we won't fail the exam.
6. After the exam Kevin and John are going to spend a week at the seaside.
   Or: After the exam Kevin and John are spending a week at the seaside.
7. When does the exam start/begin on Monday?
8. Sheila is going to visit her grandmother in India in August.
   Or: Sheila is visiting her grandmother in India in August.

11. Übungen zu allen Futurformen

52 53

Übung 1

Pat:	I've got some good news for you. Tim and I are going to go to Berkeley as exchange students for a year. And one other thing: Before we leave we are going to get married/we are getting married – on August 21st.
Pamela:	That's wonderful! I'll be your bridesmaid. That is – if you want me.
Pat:	Of course I do! You can be sure that I won't say "Yes" if my best friend is not at my side. The wedding won't be a big one. Nevertheless, there are lots of things that have to be arranged.
Pamela:	You can count on me if you need any help.
Pat:	Thanks a lot. My mother is going to write the invitations. And my brother's band is going to play at the wedding party. By the way, my 93-year-old great-grandmother is coming / is going to come, too.
Pamela:	When does the semester start at Berkeley?
Pat:	It starts exactly one week after our wedding. So we won't have much of a honeymoon!
Pamela:	Are you going to stay on campus? Or: Will you be staying on campus?
Pat:	Yes, that will make things a lot easier. By the time all our friends come visiting us we will have found places where they can stay without paying a fortune.
Pamela:	I'll miss you terribly during that year.
Pat:	So will I. But I'll be sending / 'm going to send you hundreds of postcards and e-mails.
Pamela:	When you come back, you will have got an American accent.
Pat:	Oh, no – we won't. But, listen: If you don't visit us in Berkeley, I'll be really disappointed. Oh God, it's late. I'm meeting Tim at four o'clock.
Pamela:	Well, then you'd better hurry up! Give him a kiss from me.

Übung 2

1. Nobody will have to leave the house to buy food or clothes.
2. Everything will be ordered online and delivered immediately.
3. Statements like: "Next week we are going to make / are making a trip to the moon" won't be unusual.
4. "How long will you be staying?" / "How long are you going to stay?"
5. "We are going to spend / are spending / 'll be spending three nights at the space resort. From there we are going to make / 'll be making several day trips to the moon."
6. "Excuse me, when does the next space shuttle leave?"
7. On earth the water in rivers will have become drinkable again.
8. Every pupil/student will bring his pocket computer to class. Maybe the classroom will have become a virtual one.